A must-have companion for anyone on a spiritual path.
Lee Kilburn

I love it, and I understand it was channelled in an old-fashioned way from Source. I liken The Writings *to* The Teachings of Abraham *and* A Course in Miracles. *I recommend this book as a reference and guidance tool.*
Rita-Marie Lenton
Celebrant

The Writings *are transformational. They are living wisdom that will resonate with the heart and soul of every person who reads them. They are a doorway into a new time for humanity providing each reader the opportunity to Awaken and expand their consciousness, their life, and ultimately their purpose at this time.*

And I believe they are the answer to the confusion and chaos of our world, providing an antidote of peace and spiritual nourishment as well as the Wisdom for personal awakening and enlightenment.
Josh A.

Inspiring, practical, and Loving … and very timely. A must-read for anyone interested in a Path of Self Awareness and Awakening.
Ron Hansen

THE
WRITINGS

The Writings
Copyright © 2024 The Golden Bee Enterprise
First published 2024

Disruptive Publishing
17 Spencer Avenue
Deception Bay QLD 4508
Australia
www.disruptivepublishing.com.au

Cover design and cover art by Alicia Grady
www.struckbyviolet.com

All rights reserved. Without limiting the rights under Copyright reserved above, no part of this publication may be reproduced, stored in, or introduced into a database and retrieval system, or transmitted in any form or by any means (electronic, mechanical, photocopying, recording or otherwise) without the prior written permission of both the owner of the Copyright and the above publishers.

ISBN: 978-1-7636156-9-4 Print

THE
WRITINGS

I am Pure Love that comes to you
amidst the words of your world.

I am not the words as such, but the invigorating
massage — that is beyond words — that works
the muscles of your Heart, called Pure Love.

Dedication

*The Writings are an expression of the Circle of Life.
They honor Love and Truth as the life-force of your
pure consciousness and all pure consciousness.*

*This Wisdom is dedicated to your path of awakening,
as a returning, a remembering, that you are pure as
Conscious Self. And as the pure Self you are
the Circle of Life.*

This is bowed to with the deepest honor and respect.

We dedicate this to Love that which you are.

A note to the reader

Each one of you is individual and unique.

The Writings are a personal treasure for your Awakening.

How you utilise the Wisdom is your choice. It is not a traditional book. Each of The Writings is a 'stand-alone' dialogue. So you may move about the book in whatever way you feel drawn.

Let your intuition decide.

Savour your relationship with the Wisdom in gratitude and appreciation, happiness and joy, compassion and peace.

CONTENTS

FOREWORD 1
PREFACE: THE PURPOSE OF THE WRITINGS 5
THE JOURNEY OF YOUR UNIQUE CHOICES 11
THE CALLING 19
THE EMBRACEABLE ONE 29
THERE IS NO TRUTH OUTSIDE OF LOVE 39
COMPLACENCY OR SELF-RESPONSIBILITY 47
YOU ARE FIRST, AND FOREMOST, THE BREATH 57
HARMONIZING VIEWPOINT AND VIEW 67
THE MOST INFLUENTIAL POWER IN YOUR LIFE 77
LIFE, AS THE MOTHER 87
YOUR WORLD, CONSTRUCTED AND PERFORMED 97
THE COMING OF THE GODDESS 109
AMBITION, THE DISTORTER OF THE WISDOM 123
THE FLOW OF CONSCIOUSNESS 137
LIFE ISSUES 151
UNDERSTANDING DUALITY IN GOD AS GOD 165
EVERYONE'S LIFE PATH WILL TURN A CORNER 177
THE SEEDS OF YOUR AWAKENING 189
THE FORK IN THE ROAD: YOU CHOOSE 201
SEEN THROUGH THE EYES OF KARMA 213
AM I STILL LOVED? 225

CONSCIOUSNESS IS WHAT AND WHO YOU ARE	239
YOUR GLOBAL ASHRAM	253
HARMONY OR DISHARMONY	267
YOU, AS PRECIOUS LIFE	279
THE ESSENCE OF 'I AM ONLY HUMAN'	289
YOU ARE YOUR CHRIST'S DREAM	301
THE CENTER OF THE CROSSROAD	309
"I AM THE CENTER OF LIFE"	319
THE INSTINCTUAL YOU	333
THE POWER THAT IS LOVE	347
CONCERNING THE AUTHOR	359
ACKNOWLEDGEMENTS	361
WHAT'S NEXT FROM THE SAME SOURCE?	363
CONTACT GOLDEN BEE	365

Foreword

My Beloved One,

All such Wisdom as this may be viewed as having multiple purposes. All of which are to trigger a shift in personal and global Consciousness.

There are so many choices available to you as to how you approach The Writings as a personal relationship.

As with all love affairs there has to be an initial introduction in which you want to gain an appreciation for the nature of who and what it is you are going to consider spending time with.

As with all true love affairs, you are going to embark on a journey of discovery, in which your initial focus will be on The Wisdom. But as with all great love affairs the more you find yourself wanting to know of the one you are attracted to, curious about — even mesmerized by — the more you discover yourself.

This is the nature of Love. Love is always about self-revelation. It is always the desire, the passion, the wanting to become a greater lover, and in that, the desire to have the love affair grant you a more heightened experience of Love.

The Writings and the love affair may appear to be

THE WRITINGS

outside of you, separate from you, new to you, but that is not true. The Writings—the love affair—are all going on within you, for you ... as you.

All of this you have manifested, as appearance, as the giver and the receiver, to return you to the Circle of Life that is you. To know this, to reacquaint yourself, to remember that the Circle of Life has always been present in you as you. You simply lost touch with this Truth.

You are wanting the Truth; this is how you manifested The Writings into your life. They are a reflection of what already exists and are present within you as Truth.

So, the love affair is within you—as you—as the Circle of Life. This is the most profound and precious relationship you can, and will ever, have.

It is the Love Affair called, "God I Am".

All your other relationships can be and will be fed, nurtured, and nourished by this Love Affair.

No one can teach you or train you how to be in this relationship. You must find your way. It is the way of the Heart. It is your Self Initiation into the Consciousness of Surrender, in which you will want to let go of all that you say you know, and in return sit within the Eternal Silence and be revealed to who you are.

You will have your own soul awakenings that will be

Foreword

a path of self-realization for you. A path that has never truly had a beginning and will never truly end.

Like you, as you, it is ongoing forever.

I love you.

So be it.

Preface: The Purpose of THE WRITINGS

The Writings are an expression, a truly grounded expression, on this Earth Plane, of Union Consciousness. Union Consciousness does not carry the ego state as 'only human' Separation Consciousness.

The Writings represent a more refined Consciousness which is why the 'only human' ego mind cannot grasp it and hold it as remembered, even after having just read it. And this has always been the highest intention. The Writings are not meant to be diagnosed and debated — as is the nature of the judgmental, human, opinionated mind — but rather to simply *get out of the way* and let what is 'The Flow' continue its path into you as soul consciousness.

The Writings are intended to awaken and trigger movement in your soul. Any reaction of a human nature kind is only relevant in what this indicates to you about your own connections to Separation Consciousness. This is why The Writings can be so challenging to the human self. They expose the human self, as ego, and give it no place to hide and no place in which it can truly defend itself.

As these Writings become public and enter the domain

THE WRITINGS

of third-dimensional Separation Consciousness it will be both welcomed and despised.

The Writings are not looking for a following. The Writings do not possess a personality. They do not have a figurehead to get attracted to and caught up in. The Writings simply exist as Presence, as Wisdom's display as Truth. There is Truth at levels way beyond these Writings, and that is good for all to know.

As you awaken spiritually, The Writings, as Presence, will be there to unfold the Wisdom, as Truth, at a more profound level of awareness, so that you may turn on your own Light of greater self-knowing and self-awareness.

The mysticism of The Writings is their ability to have relevance on many different layers of awakening consciously. Each word, each phrase, each sentence, each paragraph holds multiple portals that are entranceways to human and Spirit self-realization. As each person moves from only reading the words into conscious states of 'I am' awareness you will find yourself having experiences of more expanded awakenings. And for many there will be the experience of having had an awakening that may not have been fully conscious, but when you read something of The Writings you experience an 'ah ha' moment.

Such experiences occur when what has already been seeded in the consciousness from within this or

Preface: The Purpose of THE WRITINGS

another lifetime springs forth into the light of day. Such points of intense focused awareness are important in all spiritual awakening, for they come forth from a self-aware state that is greater than the 'only human' consciousness.

For this they must be treasured, written down within your own personal sacred texts, detailing your path of awakening moments. Such a sacred diary is one form of keeping track of your progress as an awakening one. This will give you opportunities to experience gratitude and appreciation for how self-responsible you are becoming, and have become, in honoring the gift of your spiritual awakening.

The Writings can become mesmerizing, even hypnotic to the human ego self. This occurs not because of the words themselves but comes from the energies of Higher Consciousness that is the source of their creation.

There is a flow to them that can be experienced if you are open enough, as personal receivership. This is the Divine Flow of Life. Life expressed as The Word, The Word that is an emanation from The Truth. In this dimension it is called Sacred Wisdom.

The Writings come, as consciousness, from within the Ecstatic state in which Love, as Light and Sound vibration, orchestrate the feeling state of ecstasy. Ecstasy is hidden in the state that The Writings hold and can be found as experience the more you

THE WRITINGS

relinquish as your known self, the 'only human' consciousness.

The Writings are an invitation to find your own path of awakening within them. The Writings belonged to no one and everyone. Once you are drawn to them and feel aligned to them, they become yours. Yours as inspiration, yours as understanding, yours as direction, and yours as your awakening spiritually, to embrace as is your soul's intent and purpose.

The Writings are a manuscript even though the way they exist as a creation from Spirit do not seem to be just one manuscript, but they are. There is only one message expressed over and over in a multiplicity of ways, viewed from this direction then that direction: from this microcosmic viewpoint to that macrocosmic viewpoint. Handing to you over and over and over the one simple message,

"Awaken, Awaken, Awaken into the Truth of the Self you are. The Self that has never been born and can never die".

Any understanding of the Self other than this is illusionary. And the world that substantiates this other self is illusionary too. You are a Consciousness of Love. You are from Source, as Beginning, and you are always this as the core and center of your existence. Your purpose, your desire, is to return to your beginning as the Original Great One you are.

What is made of this Wisdom will depend upon each individual soul's state of evolution. The purpose of

Preface: The Purpose of THE WRITINGS

this Wisdom is not to convince you of its Truth, but to simply act as a catalyst that may assist your own path upon The Way.

Wisdom such as this cannot be decided upon, one way or another. You can only sit in the Presence of it, beyond words and language, and simply inhale its resonation, vibration, and frequency, as Light and Sound, energetically.

This is how your soul is massaged, unhindered by the human mind of ignorance. It is your soul you are looking to for the movement of spiritual awakening — not your human ego heart and mind of ignorance.

Quote from *THE WRITINGS*

The Journey of Your Unique Choices

My Beloved One,

At this time, on this auspicious day, there has come forth great revelations. And in the future, they will be for you great realizations.

You have come here, at this time of great turmoil, when the appearance of everything, as normal, can be maintained by the machine that is your culture. You have come here to change what must be changed. Therefore, you and I have undertaken to bring peace as a partnership of body, mind, and soul.

You have come to assist, along with many others — the movement away from manipulation and control — to deliver life as precious, precious existence, to the hearts and minds of a humanity that already hungers and thirsts for the feelings, the sensations, and the pure knowing of this indescribable Peace.

For this Peace is not the one that waits in the wings for war to be over. Nor is it the peace that is the accumulated manufacturing of treaties, concocted so often, to deceive the heart that any other peace is possible or realizable.

You cannot continue, as a humanity, to brandish

swords of war in the name of peace, and call it evolvement, and call it dignified, in the name of Life. There is to be no further capitulation to the forces of dark manoeuvring that would have you understand the nature of your world to be what it is not.

History is history. You cannot continue to base your platform for the future upon what has already transpired. So much of the offered up evolutionary forces that you bow to as truth — that you acknowledge as authority — are no more than an orchestration of minds that perceive a destiny, and in that, a power to have what is, remain. Such a determination has little, if any, boundaries. Wanting only to infiltrate the minds and hearts of a beautiful humanity with such obscure and profound doubts that all beliefs must be born from theirs; all truth must first be bathed in theirs. And all hope springs from them.

Such decadence is the way you are being offered to yourself. Such doubt, as personal feeling, means you accept and will accept the offering. For where else is there to go when there seems so little, as an alternative offering?

For so many, the ignorance of the way is capitulated and recapitulated because you do not understand where to walk or how to walk into the arms of the miracle you call true salvation. Where true salvation is not handed to you as faith in a future, but draws you, instead, into an inner sense of how to and where to.

The Journey of Your Unique Choices

You are all looking; even the most ignorant, the most asleep, of any humanity, is still gazing through the eyes of their soul into a world before their human eyes, wanting to highlight the path that, in this moment, will springboard them into a possible allegiance.

Allegiance to the flag is well understood, as is allegiance to a country, to a faith of beliefs, to relationships of family and friends. All of these you understand. All of this, you say, is important. Importance is the sense of belonging, of being a contributor to the makeup and texture of the greatness that is perceived, the brilliance that is celebrated, and the oneness that thrives.

All such understanding and appreciation given to you have boundaries. When indeed, such a state of experience as allegiance, inside each human, can be focused anywhere and on anything. So, in your world, the ideology of separateness, is used to sew together a fabric that has each of you gazing, in dreams, at what is a very narrow, very conflicted, and competitive understanding of the greatness that Allegiance can aspire to.

There is the ideology of you as soul, that is not the conditioned or the karmically influenced one, but the Divinely inspired one you are, that is never without the consciousness, the awareness, that Life and you can reflect a greater unity of purpose. That can be the expression of a synchronized Life, of body and soul, heart and mind … Divine and human. In such a consciousness, your world would be very different. The understandings you seek would already be realized and lived as natural life.

You seek, in that state, only to create greater and greater connection to the Source that already lives and pulsates, that impassions and inspires you, that motivates and drives you. You will only want more and more, the sense of there being but the One.

All multiplicity — as Life — is sourced as the Beginning. The Beginning One, the One, the Oneness, in which there is but the One Love, the One Wisdom, the One Bliss and Rapture, the One Happiness and Joy, the One Compassion and Peace.

The One spawned Life. Life spawned greater and greater divergence. Divergence became multiplicity. Multiplicity became choice. Choice moved outwards. And now you are in the understanding of life as choice, life as an outrageous proposition.

What to do with it? *How* to do it? *Why* to do it?

Explanation became synonymous with multiplicity, for now you needed to understand journey and journey needed explaining. For so long now, in time beyond your comprehension to accept — the life you are — has wanted two things and that is to journey outwards and to journey inwards.

You are both. You live as both.

Even when you are 'asleep' as consciousness, what

The Journey of Your Unique Choices

you are aware of will mean you are—or are not—responding as the taking of action, to deliver yourself. Where deliverance says you are journeying a purpose. And that is true. You cannot and will not understand your personal journey of choices as the journey of your unique purpose until you find a need to seek peace. Peace of mind, peace in the heart, peace in relationship, peace in the family, peace upon the land and peace upon Earth. Peace can only come to you, as you begin to awaken to the certainty inside your own soul that it is all One. Everything, no matter how conflicted and convoluted it may look or actually be, began and is still, eternally, the Beginning Oneness.

Any experience, any expression that is the Play that says this is not so, is only possible in the absence of your personal surrender to, "I must return to what I truly am. I must bring my world and all that I love, and all whom I love, with me. Otherwise there is no peace".

Peace that is the compassion. Compassion that is the realization that there is no peace without it. And without it, "I am sentencing myself to the sleep of incessant conflict, where dreams are dreams of confusion. Where confusion harbors danger, and danger fosters belief in enemies. And enemies birth defense, and defense births attack. And attack births war, and war births the loop of vigilant separateness, as truth".

And that truth keeps the heart and the mind of many

humans in a state of longing, in a state of hoping and wishing for what never seems to arrive for the one, for the whole, as a peace-filled humanity.

It is no longer enough to have personal peace. The drug, the relationship, the holiday, no matter the fix or fixation that for the moment tastes of temporary peace, it will be seen only as a band-aid for a wound that never heals. The lack of peace is the great wound, the personal wound, that afflicts humanity. A life without peace is life as a wound. Life as a wound is a life that is always seeking to heal that wound. The search for anything, the search for everything within a human life, is the search for peace.

The elusive Beginning you are. The Peace you are. You are more than a humanity lost to peace. You are more than the restless human soul, human spirit, that does not know what it truly seeks; cut off and blind, cut off and deaf, unable to speak, unable to call out, unable to hear, so dense is the confusion.

Whatever you have been told that speaks to you of there being no Oneness: of all diversity, all multiplicity transcending into Source, being untrue. Of all cycles being a part of greater cycles and all ages a part of greater ages. Of all groups being part of greater groups and all families a part of a greater one. Each soul — and all souls — are part of greater and greater groups of souls. All consciousness, at one level is part of greater and greater levels of consciousness. And the parts that make up the whole, all converge on the Source, at the

The Journey of Your Unique Choices

Source, as the One, The Beginning.

To consider the expansion of your own understanding, to transcend the consciousness of multiplicity with all the inherent mental and emotional problems that you find yourself drowning in, is only possible when you give to yourself the Truth that we are One, we are One, we are One.

And no matter how different—and even the very opposite—your life may look like as your personal journey, keep reminding yourself of this Truth over and over and over. And then you will, with time, begin to realize if it is not so, then what is not making it so? What is holding that Truth from becoming a reality, as your visible, audible world, as life upon your Earth?

You are already awakening. You are already coming into realizations that what you most need, and will therefore find, is that priceless path of life called the Journey Home. And when you realize that this is what you truly seek, you will then remind yourself every day, and every night before you sleep, that all and any conflict in your personal life and life in the world around you, will only be resolved with greater peace.

And so, the journey becomes an expression of your openness to the path of peace. All experience is your quest to have it *resolve* as peace, and that it *results* in peace. All journey, all experience is begun in peace. And if at any time, conflict presents itself, it is only to speak, "I am *of* peace, I am *for* peace, I *am* peace."

THE WRITINGS

Continue to march, continue to journey. Do not feel the need to enter the grounds of conflict. Do not respond to the energies of the not-peaceful that may be conjured and then harnessed from within you.

Speak only:

"I am peace, you are peace, we are peace. If that cannot be realized now, in this moment, let us come together again later, when peace is upon my heart and yours, when peace is in my mind and yours, when peace is the taste of my words and yours, when I know in advance, that the outcome is peace. For that is what I am. That is the meaning of life for me. You are in my life; therefore, you are peace to me. I pray this for you, to you, for I love you always."

I love you.

So be it.

The Calling

My Beloved One,

I bless you now as you walk upon your path towards those days to come that have now arrived and are arriving. You never imagined that they would arrive so quickly because you, at that time, were looking into a future through eyes that were filled with a different time and a far different reflection than what now is becoming apparent as life on Earth today.

You are living in times when the future is being made manifest, when all that has been spoken of is now taking place as preparation, as the first obvious signs, one upon another, that leads you to view the Light of Life at work upon your world. Yes, it is true that it has been in existence, as Existence, here forever, but these are the days when Light is expressed through the hands and the mouths of the many. When words are spoken, and actions are taken that are the inspiration that affirms the goodness that lives here as humanity renewed.

Recovering from the devastation that has for so long been agreed upon by those who would be that kind of decision maker, lost as they have been to the tenacity with which life holds to Life. Your world has been

THE WRITINGS

unwilling to completely succumb to the rubble of consciousness that speaks more of despising and conflict, which has upheld as relevant the constant need to compare. And in that, find fault and blame — if only to prepare an innocent world for steps that would become actions that would be the escalation of violence into domains of life that was never conceived of by this Earth plane and its peoples.

But you have continued — as life — to gravitate towards ease, even when ease for you has not been well thought out in terms of what is best and highest for your precious bodies, and your precious hearts, and minds. That kind of ease — as decision making — has brought to you great difficulty, for it allowed you to rely upon others whom it has now been shown — and will in fact further be shown — should not have been relied upon.

Such an understanding of ease came to you in your lethargy and from that perspective it seemed the best solution. But lethargy, you are now understanding, is a corruption of Life and a dissolving of life force. Your precious will to live, inherent in you from the Beginning is weakened and dissipated, and in that you are made incapable as humanity to truly take responsibility for how you want your world to look and be, and how you want it to taste and feel to the consciousness.

You now are beginning to appreciate, on another level of awareness, that you cannot continue to escalate

The Calling

your own level of 'not responsible' and then complain when the outcomes in your world, as your world, are not as you want or wanted. So, to turn all this around is the process you are now engaging in, from the very incidental, in your eyes, to the gravely important in the eyes of an awakening humanity.

It matters little what your continuously reactive conscious mind is doing. None of it has any relevance when placed before your budding commitment to ignore it all in your quest to remain seated in the state of peace. And all that that looks like and feels like as the Life you want to live within: the relationship exchanges you long to have and the ethnic multiplicity of the true One Soul you are as a unified humanity. You are looking to uplift a world that will precipitate a shift in the consciousness of this world, the likes of which is unimaginable in your present state of awareness, but will become the inauguration of the one Great Blessing that will touch Life everywhere. Such is the Becoming, as a path of awakening, that you are upon.

I have spoken before of such matters, and you may well ask,

"What is different now?"

And I say to you, "You are".

It is you that has changed and is changing. Your connection to everyone and everything is becoming more real to you, more tangible. And in that, you find a mindfulness and a heartfelt desire to be the Change that is the Calling: soul *to* soul, soul *upon* soul, soul *within* soul—there is now the one resonation. There is the fire to seed the Consciousness of greater with more refined expressions and experiences of the one Life you are.

In the Heavens and upon the Earth this calling resonates and vibrates and tunes the soul of each and every life expression to gather.

"Gather yourselves, each and every one of you, and beckon as that Calling to have the seed of the One Life grow from within your soul."

You are looking to germinate and water, to nurture and protect this Calling, for it is in the profoundest state of your consciousness: You calling to you, the Divine calling to the human, the All calling to a one.

Your conviction that this is the Truth must overcome the lethargy instilled into the conscious mind of you—as human. Such is the nature of this disease that it can look like anything and still seed death in the consciousness. Whether it be greed or power, insensitivity or shame, every human will find that lethargy—as opinion, as purpose, as perspective—is driving your life. It may not look like it to you because you have defined your lives on so many levels with the definition and determination of success. But all such pathways have come to you as an urging from within that is in some way founded upon lethargy.

The Calling

Lethargy says,

"In this moment, in this area of my life I am not, cannot, will not be the greatest, highest, life expression I can be".

So, lethargy stands as you, between you and your Self as an Enlightened One, as an Awakened One. Your path as an awakening one is to cleanse and purify all of the beliefs that are actions of habit that you define as you and the life you are.

To be in your comfort zone is really nothing more than your subconscious and conscious adoption of thoughts and behaviours that were spawned from your original emotional state of self-rejection. This emotional state became you at the earliest of ages, as a child, as doubt was awakened consciously within you and the 'I am' awareness moved from its natural state of Being into the convoluted world of pain and suffering in which everything became something to decide upon.

"Will I embrace this, will I not?"

"Will I reject you or accept you?"

"Will you hurt me or support me?"

"Will you want my life to embrace as something wonderful, or hold me away at arm's length?"

Everything in this world—as consciousness—is confusion, felt or unfelt, acknowledged or not. In each life the same process exists.

THE WRITINGS

The time is now, when all of this will be changed as each human is challenged by their willingness to accept that none of this acquired persona of lethargy is you or has anything to do with who you really are as original you, as a natural one, as your true and perfect nature. As that, you are Love. And within that consciousness you express yourself as happiness and joy, as compassion and peace. In that, you are the humble and bowed allowance of all life. All life its journey, all life its lessons, all life its realizations, all life its path, brilliantly walked as the Circle of Life into the remembering of, "I am all that I am".

And in that announcement, your 'heart of compassion' places forgiveness there upon the Altar of Life to be taken up as sacred and wholly precious as the great key for alignment: alignment to the Self, and alignment towards all others and all life.

Forgiveness says, "I surrender the explanation".

To surrender the explanation allows you to awaken yourself to the disease of lethargy held in you as human nature.

This awakening re-ignites the fire of Will that penetrates the wall of illusion called your acquired human mind, and seeds dreams of a greater you, a greater life, and a greater world.

And within your newly-awakened heart of compassion, you know you are an instrument of life that now inspires others, that now reflects brilliantly

The Calling

to others that you are, and they are, the Great One being reborn.

Reborn as awakening, opens to you, as consciousness, the experience of an already existing world that is the consciousness of Light. You realize you are returning as human consciousness to the state of Merging, in which all, as the one Life, is the one Divine everything.

And you begin from your heart and your mind, filled as they are with compassion, with tolerance and forgiveness, with a deeply held respect for the preciousness of life. All life to create visions of Earth as you want this life to be, how you want humanity to be, how you want all life to be treated here.

And so, each and all of you, with your own particular sensitivities to life, with all of your personal heartfelt dreams for uplifted actions, uplifted words and feelings, uplifted creations, mirror and reflect how much you love life, all life, every one's life, everything as life. Where all exchanges, all giving and receiving reflect the one connectivity, the one changeable and the one unchangeable through which this connectivity flows. And allowances are recognized as necessary as you consider through your heart of compassion the need to accept that everyone will awaken eventually, and in their changing, will incorporate their own dreams into the existing fabric of awakening consciousness and its visions of a new world.

There is so much to comprehend that has not yet been

given to you, but there is a future now in which you will exist, where you will find ease and acceptance of such understandings. You will then become the teachers, the compassionate ones of Light that will be the torch bearers for those who are still 'Becoming'.

And as you breathe you are aware, more and more, that you can sustain yourself as consciousness, as awareness, in the states of Time and No Time. And this connectivity is the coming-to-fruition of your own dreams, your own aspirations, that for so long have wanted this to be so. And here it is now, and you call it your awakening, and you had no idea that it would look like this and feel like this. And you will speak this again, over and over, as you enter into greater and greater levels of awakening. And each is a petal in the flower of your Enlightenment.

Each holds you as achievement, and each holds you as potential. For in each petal there is the seed: the seed that begets the flower. And in that beginning there are each of your new beginnings, as the steps you took that became your next achievement. The next achievement that becomes the next potential, never ending, circles within circles, upon circles, infinitely expanding as you expand. And will you ever find an ending in which all that you achieved, all that was the potential, culminates, concludes, ends?
This cannot be known unless you may speak, "Beyond this achievement there is no potential to expand into further achievements."

The Calling

But Life is not this way. God is not this way. Father, Mother Existence cannot be this way. Eternal is eternal, unending is unending, forever is forever, and ongoing is ongoing. Where is there not Love? This is what will drive you, thrive you into, "I must know that answer. I must have it as 'I am'. I must be it."

And so, the flower and the seed, achievement and potential, reach on and on into configurations beyond the human mind's ability to grasp. And in that, it falls silent into a dreamless sleep. And in that, you have forged a thought, like an arrow sent from a bow that flies forever into realms of Life and Light. Attached to the bow that is held by the archer is a golden, white, silver string of Light that holds, as Love, the Song of the Father, the Beat of the Mother.

"*Come, come, come this way, this way, this way.*"

The Calling, the Eternal Song.

I love you.

So be it.

The Embraceable One

My Beloved One,

I have come to you upon a gliding ship of Light. I have come to you as the sweet scent of a victory you thought you could never win. I come to you and speak to you from a space so close, as if I was standing on the tip of your nose. I come to you and say, "It is time now. It is time to move, a time to be what you have come to be. You understand Love, you understand Light. Now it is time to exist as that in your life."

You may call yourself sweet and special, and that is reasonable, for all that is of Life is known as that. You are gazed upon from the Heavens that are all around you and inside you too. It is the appreciation of a Beginning and a Belonging that has never left you. But still, you tantalize yourself with understandings of a history that has no compensations. That guarantees you nothing of what it is you truly seek, as that which you truly are.

There have been times in your life when I have watched you so closely to bring to your awareness, the Presence, of that which I be. I have stood before you and said to you, "Awaken."

THE WRITINGS

To achieve this, you must look at what you say you cannot see. But here I am, as that which you be, which is true and the same for all of humanity. It is the beginning of a 'knowing' that will walk with you forever as you walk through every lifetime. You cannot help but realize there is within you a knowing that I exist, and I am the ever-present one you are.

There is a One that is before each of you, as humanity, which is called the 'I' that is your true Self. It is the one that holds the One Beginning for you, and is *within* that One *as* *t*he One. And each of you will speak, as that One, "I am individual and I am unique". And you say, "I am."

This, your 'I am', is the force, the power that must be acknowledged over and over. The simplicity of 'I am' is all that is needed, all that is required. You can never come upon yourself, as the Self, without this understanding. Speak, "I am" and leave it as a Beginning. Leave it as your knowing that there is a 'you' that can never truly awaken without Self-appreciation.

In time, Self-appreciation will lead you to an acceptance that there is a greatness within you that you can express through many human endeavors, many human undertakings. There is a need to place yourself within the flow of this energy within you. There is not a moment of time when it is not possible to touch the greatness you are. For it is experienced when you live within your life as one that is entranced.

The Embraceable One

You feel within you this amazing life-force that says to you, "Arise my life, make it greater."

And it speaks to the 'you' that wants that, but is afraid, or baffled, or confused. It speaks to the 'you' that only has a past to consider when looking at its future. Do not look back to where you have come from other than to appreciate it for what it has given you. Or what it has not, that you still need to gain as experience, as your journey through time.

There is a 'you' to become that does not live within the shadows of life or within the afterglow of someone else's striving, someone else's ambition. Life is yours to have, and it will take you wherever you feel to go. Life does not lead you, unless that is your perception. Life is so filled with treasure, so filled with blessings, so filled with all that can be appreciated. You have to understand who you are in your life. You have to know who you are in Life itself.

Your life can be many things. It depends upon how much you have, over time, in any lifetime, come to appreciate that life is a garden filled with delight. If nothing is judged, then nothing is not of the garden. If all is allowed in your life, then it will have something to offer. There is never in anyone's life, no matter how it appears to anyone else, a garden that is not filled with opportunities to appreciate, to have gratitude, to be filled with thanks.

And you may wonder what is it that allows the human

to become the grateful one, to begin a life of appreciation?

You, my blessed one, as the child, lived in a world of purity that spoke of fascination and wonderment. There was nothing that was not able to be felt through the eyes, the smell, the taste, and the touch. All things carried a knowing, all things were a receiving.

"Come to me, precious life."

That is the pure consciousness of the baby and innocent child. To never let go of the lightness of being that enabled you to exist as the one that loves life. There is always the fascination, always the curiosity. That is what will lead you back to a world of Love. To be the human who is the adult, is to have lost that, except in moments of awaked-ness, when all that is your world has fallen away as an encumbrance, and once again you live in the simple moment of appreciation.

Your world can never be appreciated in the mind. But the mind will tell you that it can. There is the simple joy and wonderment that speaks of what the eyes can see, what you can smell and taste, what you have heard and can hear again. This is your reservoir of life. What you sense is what you feel. You can live life as a hunger that speaks, "I must have more."

Everything is a seeking to have more. That is what you must tell yourself. For you know this already. It lies within you as Love. As love of your life and to love

The Embraceable One

that you live. That you awaken each day to a life that you want, to a life that you have, that can only get better, can only be greater. This must be your lust. This must be your passion.

There is a temperature within you that rises the more you feel the passion for life, and it will activate your pineal center and the pituitary center, particularly. But all your centers of Life that exist within you, that identify for you the realization of, 'I am', in its many different facets, and in its many different realizations, will awaken.

Life is a realized thing. You can never appreciate all that you call, 'my life' until you free yourself from the web of intrigue you call conditioning. There is not one of you who does not have a created understanding and a created appreciation. It is a doorway that exists for you, that separates the life 'I am' that is your conditioning, and the Life 'I am' that speaks:

"I am liberated. I am free. I am exuberant and I am elated. I am held captivated in the sheer awesomeness of Life itself."

And it is yours and it is you, and you seek to know this. As you push for that awakening, it will come to you as you strive to free yourself from the shackles and the burdens of life called 'conditioned'. And you will know it when you are feeling these 'flights of freedom' for they will feel to you — outrageous and demanding in their desire for expression — liberating in their sense of doing, and elation at their time of completion. It will become addictive. There will be the 'I' that is you, that wants this more.

And this 'I' that is you, that expresses this liberation, is an already-existing you. And you know you can feel it and sense it. You may wonder, how? and why? You can now be told that this 'you' is born with such a thirst, such a hunger. This you, as the 'Christed One' is an already existing One of Light. It is the 'you' that carries the demand for Life that is the passion of the Beginning One. It is the wholesome one that is the Beginning that is the Creator Power that carries the Father, the Mother, which is all Life as the One.

And so, you have unlocked—and so, you have unleashed—the Sacred One you are, the One that is moved by all of Life, the One who knows of its own Existence within all of Life. The Christed One plays upon a landscape created that is of its own understanding, its own Truth. Miracle upon miracle can be set upon your world when the Christ, that which is the within of you, that is the without of you, begins to weave a magic that is the destiny of all Life.

The magic that speaks, "We are of the one God, therefore, you and I as everything and anything in Life, can be felt, both as a *within* and a *without*. All can be altered, all can be changed, all can be manifested, for it is pliable, as created, to that which created it".

To be a Christed One is to hold the Creator Power of

The Embraceable One

the Divine Father and Divine Mother. And as that Power, as the Love, all can be seduced to fulfil all purposes, all destinies. Miracles laid upon a platform called human existence are what the world awaits. And there are those upon this plane of existence who will weave magic that you will know to be the miracle. For life that was once an expression created will arise, as if in a new life upon a new plane of expression.

And how did this occur? You will wonder, and that curiosity will birth for you the desire to know. This will bring forth the Christed One within you, that has but one desire, and that is to be the existing 'you' upon this your Earth. To not be the hushed and silent one, but the ever-present one of Light, who has now attached the Self, as consciousness, to human form. And with that has brought to life its God.

And you know that such a one will begin to orchestrate life here in a way that is profound and responsible. It will begin to assume the responsibility that you will all embrace, as you walk toward your destiny as the one who is Christed, the one who is the Buddha. And in this Becoming, you will seed for others upon your plane, the understanding of:

"I am my own destiny. I am that which I seek. There is no other. All was a stepping-stone. All was an announcement to awaken the One."

So, you set out upon your journey each day and you call it your path. And it is seen as a path of joy and happiness, as a path that requires of you the sweet felt understandings of compassion and peace. And you will know, through experience, that you cannot walk away from any experience without a feeling of, "I am deserting myself. I am abandoning my life."

Never let any experience overwhelm you to this extent. Even though for many of you it already has. This is not an answer. It is a solution dreamt up in the mind and heart of pain and it cannot, and will not, offer you who you are and what you seek.

"I am the Embraceable One." This is what you must say to yourself, over and over, until you begin to have that sweet sensation of 'knowing' that you are. And that you can embrace all of what has been, and is to be, your human life.

The forgotten tides of memories await your coming as the accepting principle of your Christ, the compassionate heart of yourself the Buddha.

You will walk here as one that reaps its own harvest. For every seed you ever planted, as thought and as feeling that grew into its own brilliant expression, awaits you now to harvest it, and take from it the seed.

The seed, the seed, the seed of life, it is always the same.

"I love that I live, I love my life, I love God."

You are that. Now you may go forth, as an anointed one of Light, who seeks to have that be the true

The Embraceable One

expression of the 'you' who walks in the body human upon this Earth plane.

I love you.

So be it.

There is no Truth outside of Love

My Beloved One,

How is it that such a one as you has arrived at an understanding in which you speak of your God, as Life, as your life most specifically? And in that, there is the knowing that all Life is your life, for all that is life before you, is who you are as Life within you.

There is but little difference between the two. It is only the visuals of one that appear to outweigh the other in significance and importance. And that is as it was intended when viewed through the eyes of your human body, when heard through the ears of your human body, when felt by the touch that is human, the taste and the smell that is you, as human.

It is, however, that such a registration of life, through the body human, was never meant to be the final measuring stick by which you would assume an understanding of all Life. It is that the body was only intended to grant appreciation of life, as God, as all things, in a particular way. That is all.

To register is to prove and to prove is to experience and that is what you have before you. Experience. All of life is there to be experienced. All of it is you as an unknown. All of it comes from the within of you. All of it knows you as Source, as Beginning.

How wondrous it is that you are this Beginning. What a joy it is for you to behold yourself in this understanding and be able to embrace it in joy and belonging, to be able to embrace it in the arms of Love. Such a one is you as human who knows of Home, that is not within this realm you call human. And it is not that your home in this human realm does not have value, but that there is a greater Home, and it is felt within the state called joy, it is felt in the lovemaking that says:

"I love that I live, I love my life."

For such a one is in love with all Existence. And in the energy, the flow of that Existence, there is the ecstasy of Love. And you know this as making love. The ecstasy of the moment that you call "I love". And it is placed upon the one before you. It is a flow that moves backwards and forwards between the two and there is never a doubt, for what is known is that all that is before you, as love, as loved, will freely flow towards the you that is 'in love'.

For such a movement is the natural flow of all Life, such is the flow and the movement of all true Love. It only never looks like that or feels like that in a human, when the eyes are the eyes of rejection, when the mouth is the power of pain. When eyelids never close upon an experience that cannot be forgotten. And when the ears are pierced with screams of unwellness. This is your lot, as human, when there is pain, when there is separation, when there is ignorance and the stepping aside from all that comes to you as life.

It is not worth stepping aside from any aspect of your life, for all of it is a treasure, all of it will grant you your kingdom of Love, all of it will bless you with the feeling called Home, for all of it comes from and will return to, all that you will discover as Home. There is no thing that can be separated from the whole. There is no thing that cannot be viewed through the eyes of enchantment. For indeed, all that is before you exists — also forever — in the 'land of enchantment'. And such a one, such a vision as that, is never far away from anyone or anything that you see before you or feel within you.

Your perception is all that stands between your knowing of enchantment and your reality. For you to realize all that is your vision of life is but an illusion of thought and feeling. It exists in your mind, and it exists in your emotions. That is all. And if you were to change your mind, and your emotions, into the state of Self then you would recognize all that is before you as merely a song from a singer, a dance from a dancer, who did it all in pain.

There is no pain. There is no pain. There is no pain. It is an illusion of the mind created from an emotion. It is a dancer dancing to a tune that is felt as pain. That is felt, felt, felt in the never letting go. Pain is felt in the never letting go. You are more than what you are as 'the never letting go'.

You are brilliant Light. You are the luminescent glory of God. You are the One. You live as Self within realms of beauty that are beyond qualification and beyond judgment. You live within an 'enchanted land' where all around you is Love and all around you is the vision of Love. And that world is not beyond you now. It is before you now. Look at it again, not through the eyes of pain, but the eyes of Life, the eyes of Love.

You have never been more fortunate or more blessed than you are right now for there is an Opening in your timing, when all that has been misunderstood will be understood, and all that is from beyond the state called human, will come to you. And you will know that there is, from within the state called human, the opportunity to realize the scope of your existence, which is profound beyond measure. And in that awakening you will know your Beginning Home. You will know that all of what has been journeyed in your world has been just that, a journey.

I speak to you now about the abundance of Life and it is important that you realize and recognize that you are the One that is the many. You are the parts that are the whole. You are Existence and that which sustains It. You are Love and the lovers. You are all of It. There never has been a separation in the Garden between your Self and the Father Mother Source. For all that is

There is no Truth outside of Love

in the Garden lives within you as Home. All that is within you that is the Garden, is before you as Life, as Love, as the Beginning. It is the state of precious Existence that exists within Time and beyond Time. It is the 'Isness' that is All. And in the forever-ness of Life, and the forever-ness of you, there is the state of 'Am-ness'. That is *what* you are. You are the state of Am-ness. And in that, there is reflection and in reflection there is you and there is I. There is Life. There is ongoing-ness and there is brilliant Light. And all that exists in your world is brilliant Light. It is the Light of the One that is the Beginning.

You are never far away from Truth. It exists within every moment as a chalice, as a cup of exquisite Light, exquisite Life, and all that you drink is the Light, is the Life of Truth. There is but the One. It is the one Truth, to which all truth ascends. It is not that you need to understand the one Truth in your human mind, but begin to access it within your human heart. For Love is the flavor of the one Truth and all Truth is flavored with Love. There is the one Power that is within the one Truth, that is all Truth, that is Love. There is no Truth outside of Love. There is no Power outside of Love. All is within the within that is Love.

I come to you at this time to touch you again and again, over and over, with Love. Let it be that you understand that all of what is touched upon, all of what is spoken of, all of what is revealed, is Love. There is nothing, nothing outside of the Allowance that is Love. Be open to the realization that Love is the Power of all Existence. It is the Light of all Life. It is the great Permission. It is the great Allowance.

There is nothing in all of Life that you need view as being outside of Love, outside of Permission, outside of Allowance. All is within the Divine Hands; all is within the golden glow of Permission accepted and all is within the path of Allowance. Come now into a realization that the uplifting of all Life is brought about as a consequence of Permission and Allowance.

It is for you now to view your world and begin to speak to it, and for it to speak to you of Permission and Allowance. For in that, you will move what is before you into a state of Love. And in that, all that is before you can uplift to a greater expression. Bathe your world in Permission and Allowance. Seek to reveal to yourself all that is not yet accepted, all that lacks your permission for its life and for its expressions and experience of Life. To lack that allowance, will not uplift your 'land of enchantment', that is your life.

Remember that your garden, your 'land of enchantment' is, firstly, all that is before you bathed in Light, bathed in Love. It will be your eyes that will see the Light and feel the Love. It will be your ears that hear sweet songs of Love. It will be your heart that bathes your world in Love. Your Being, filled with Life, filled with Love, will reveal to you the 'land of enchantment' that is before you. Seek to fulfil yourself in this 'land of enchantment'. Seek to bring fulfilment

There is no Truth outside of Love

to others. Never lose sight of this realm of Love. It is within you, and it is there before you, in every moment.

Call to Love and it will come. Speak, "I want Love".

And it will come. Touch and speak:

"Let my touch be the touch of Love. Let that which I touch be Love that returns to me. I am Love and I am loved. I speak of a world before me that knows only Love. I speak from a world within me that knows only Love."

And in that, you will grant yourself all realizations you seek to have. Love will passion you for greater realizations, and in that, you will expand and expand. All that is before you will be known as You. You that is Love that is Self. And in that Movement, there will be endlessness as the 'land of enchantment' you seek to know as 'Life I am'.

Let this be an Inspiration for you. Let it bring you into greater and greater experiences of Love.

That is who we are, you and I. We are Love, and in that we are the One.

I love you.

So be it.

Complacency or self-responsibility

My Beloved One,

If you were involved in an extraordinary pursuit of something that was highly valued and greatly prized, it is without doubt that the determination you would display would be beyond comparison. For what you seek is unique and different and greatly worth the effort. Many of you as humans have placed yourselves or found yourselves in this position.

Sometimes the prize is well understood and extremely obvious. For others it is more the unknown that is anticipated. You will find, in either situation, that you are being confronted with your own sense of unbelievable purpose. To be caught in such a vortex of energy is to be described by some as fanatical. Not in terms of the beliefs you hold, as in the case of one you would term a zealot, but fanatical in that it occupies so much of your attention.

If you were to relax at all, you feel that what you are after will slip from your grasp and, therefore, you would falter in its eventual capture as your fulfilment. To capture such a thing is to move into the experience of oneness with, and in that, the taste of what that experience is like. At first there is no comparison. The very newness of the taste satisfies your whole attention. And there are so many ways, so many experiences, you gather to taste this thing. And as you acquire this taste, you become more relaxed with it, more accepting now, less 'on it' as you would say, then until, at last, it becomes accepted as a natural part of your life and who you are.

There are so many ways you have all come to experience this. In essence, it is a process of life, of living, that is utilized by every human. So too is the aspect called 'taking for granted'.

'Taking for granted' occurs when you have lost sight of the importance and significance of 'this' in your life, whatever it may be. You slip into a state of complacency that suggests that what you have will always remain with you. It becomes like a second skin to you. You become convinced that this will always be with you now. Complacency is the acceptance of what is, in a state of little or no effort and input. Where the requirement of relationships becomes minimal and is significant, as action and behaviour, only as a result of operating in a 'shared space'.

There are so many levels, so many ways, that this occurs for you. You may recognize it most clearly in your relationships with each other. You may clearly see it in your relationship with life, with your Mother Earth, with all that is life that is natural *to* your world, and *in* your world. But few of you really take the time to view it in relationship to yourself.

Complacency or self-responsibility

How do you take yourself for granted?

If you simply looked at what enters you and what moves from you, there is a whole world to see. When the entering is not just the body, but also the mind and the emotions: What you take in and take on? What you digest? What you eliminate? What you put forth into your world? The human that is body, mind, and emotions has become a processing factory that has, as a beginning, the raw products that will be used to package this 'you' that you will project to the world.

Complacency occurs in this scenario when what is going in and what is going out is not 'quality-controlled' by you.

The 'you', that is called 'the factory', is leaving the running of it up to other aspects of your consciousness. This consciousness has many names and many identities. All of which exist as a 'you' but are *not* you. This occurs as a sense of being out of sync with, of being not present totally, of not really being in the boardroom with yourself.

There are so many 'callings' within you that you experience every day, that want a part of you, that want your attention, and want to manipulate your direction. Every day your world presents thousands of directions to move into and towards. These directions you call your life, your habits, your lifestyle, your responsibilities, your cravings, your addictions, your compulsions, your dreams, your ambitions, your drives, your world and your life. And all of it — as you — is 'the factory'.

All this moves in and through and out of you as this processing plant, this 'factory'. You are there for sure. You wander around and through it, meeting with different supervisors, different department heads, but you never get to sit in the boardroom, in the chair of the CEO or president. So, you wander around 'the factory' like a homeless one, without any real sense of direction or feeling of what your purpose is. You know you cannot abandon this 'factory'; you know that it is yours.

But what is your role? What is your function within it? You know that you are supposed to be overseeing the whole operation, but you do not feel like the overseer. If you do have power and influence it is not obvious to you or apparent to anyone else. All that you do is allowed. No one says, "You do not belong here".

To have a life such as this is the outcome of complacency. And so, complacency says, "I am not responsible".

To not be responsible allows all things to be taken for granted. All things that are taken for granted become a life of their own, moving about with little focus and little leadership.

Continuity in such a circumstance is not the focus of the many working as one. But more, the many working at the same time, with no apparent direction,

Complacency or self-responsibility

and accepting it as the way it is, as the way it has to be, as your life.

So, continuity is itself redefined by complacency. So too is responsibility. For now, responsibility is the acceptance of the muddle and the lack of direction whilst not making a fuss or being alarmed. The redefining is itself necessary, as part of normalizing this situation. The normalizing allows 'what is' to exist as status quo unquestioned. This then allows complacency and 'taking for granted', to be seen as normal human behaviour. Normal human behaviour then can largely exist unchallenged.

In such a scenario of human existence, there is nothing to redeem, there is nothing lost. And complacency is allowed to write its own history and rewrite the old, for complacency must. Because history speaks of legacy, legacy speaks of a beginning. Complacency speaks, "What is has always been".

And within complacency, memory and knowing become dulled. Complacency discards the truth and creates its own version and its own vision, its own understanding of 'truth'. And so 'the factory' you wander through is a 'factory' of complacency. You, in your state of complacency, are taken for granted and have given up the ownership of your 'factory' as self. For all the things that may be spoken concerning the nature of complacency, the most significant is the removal of ownership. Where ownership is the conscious awareness of "I am."

THE WRITINGS

As 'the factory', you are unaware you are its owner. You are unaware you are its president and CEO, its founder and its creator. To no longer have a sense of ownership allows much of what enters, and much of what passes, to do so without your conscious intent. Remembering that conscious intent is not the aimless wanderings of you around the 'factory floor' and through its offices. That kind of meandering certainly can give you 'awareness of', but awareness in such circumstances is not hands-on. Hands-on says, "I know because I am."

Such awareness allows you to speak truly of being the master of your 'factory' and the master of your domain.

To speak, "I must become the master of what is outside my factory coming into my factory," is not the way. Such a suggestion as a truth — as a way — is given to you by complacency acting as the CEO and president of your 'factory'. Because it knows that any conscious objection that arises around the existing status quo must be redirected to one of complacency's major truths that you now accept as normal and true.

It speaks: "If you want to change the factory go out there and change what is coming *into* the factory."

Gone you are. Complacency smiles a knowing smile. You left your 'factory' on a crusade to change the world. And of course, complacency waved goodbye with promises of continuing to run your 'factory' for you, keeping everything normal, as it has always done.

Complacency or self-responsibility

Now you have bought into a great and successful sleight of hand, executed by complacency everywhere upon your world. For to create a normal-ness, around such a sleight of hand, allows a righteousness to develop. And righteousness is the power gained from looking outwards.

Looking outwards becomes your crusade, designed by complacency, to remove you from ever focusing on your 'factory'. Complacency wants you to limit, in regard and importance, any need you may have to take more care of what is going on in 'the factory'. And so, a great illusion is born and is maintained by the power of complacency. The illusion, carried on the wings of righteousness, speaks:

> *"Change the world, change the world,*
> *change the world."*

Noble and great are the visions born that way. Great expense has not been spared in the unfolding of these visions. And within the visions, aspirations are formed that can be embraced by a whole humanity wanting to change the world.

Wanting to alter the world outside your 'factory', as your crusade, will endure for a lifetime. And all the while complacency lives unchallenged within 'the factory'. And you never suspect that such an outcome was what was always desired. It was always known that it would occur. Complacency always speaks, "Let others be responsible."

THE WRITINGS

Complacency always feels burdened by self-responsibility. Complacency carries its own banner of 'freedom'. It has its own 'badge of courage'. It has its own 'commendations'. For complacency rewards effort placed into the pursuit of life that took you from its own doorstep. That took you from its own reflection. That upheld the truth of complacency's illusions.

All of this is your world that wants peace. All of this in a world that wants love and all of this in 'the factory of self' that you once owned as Conscious Self. It was your inability to create peace and love on the 'factory floor', in the offices of the department heads that made you complacent to begin with. Until eventually complacency was given everything by your simple withdrawing from self-responsibility:

> *"There is no love, there is so little peace.*
> *I am not responsible. I withdraw."*

And each time you did, complacency stepped up to the plate and spoke, "Leave this to me."

And you did. And so, your life becomes a thing of, "I am not responsible. I have left that up to others."

In that mood, things in life that come and go are all the result of other people's doings and their failed responsibilities. Therefore, you may take it all for granted.

There is, however, the lack of responsibility, the being taken for granted, and the complacency that existed

Complacency or self-responsibility

here on this Earth plane long before you came into the body. There was already an existence within humanity of many 'factories' with absentee owners in which complacency and 'taking for granted' happily ruled, in which there was a substituting of one focus for another. From within you, to what is outside of you, creating the ever-present consequences of complacency.

You cannot change your world through the simple crusade of righteousness. Peace, that is lasting, was never the focus of such crusades. They are there to simply uphold for you your own beliefs borne out of complacency. The beliefs that speak,

> *"Let us change what is out there. That is enough.*
> *Let us leave what is within alone."*

Such an approach will ensure the crusade continues. And in that spirit, there will always be a 'them and us'. There will always be a 'higher ground'. There will always be 'integrity' birthed in righteousness and there will always be a 'just cause'. All the while, a lifetime's energy is expended in such devotion. And little, if any, was ever used to focus upon your own 'factory' and on what comes in and what goes out.

There will never be a lasting peace until the crusader returns home to its own estate. For there, it will find a state of great neglect. And what else was there to expect? For complacency never said that it would take care to uphold the beauty and magnificence of your

THE WRITINGS

grand estate. Complacency only ever says, "Leave it to me."

'Leave it to me', says "I will neglect."

So now you are at that significant gateway of awareness. You gaze upon the life of the crusader, and you feel the Call to return to your 'factory', to your own estate, that is yourself. You are beckoned from both sides and both sides are calling to you. You do not have to decide either/or, for to return to the 'factory floor' will now allow you to begin to master the chaos that is complacency's rule.

Take your time. Do not be alarmed. You are never alone. All that you are is being returned to you.

I love you.

So be it.

You are first, and foremost, the Breath

My Beloved One,

When you 'pass your body' in any lifetime, you are at that quintessential moment when you know the meaning of transition. When you know that you are the movement in consciousness that is in the hands of a greater reality.

It is remarkable how transition occurs without you ever being conscious of instigating it. You simply glide, as awareness, into another state of being. It is as if it was a familiar and a known thing. But how could that be? How could it be planned, expected, and natural when you say you had no previous awareness? How could you go somewhere you were not sure even existed? How could you become something you had not consciously imagined? How can that all be in existence as if simply awaiting your return? As if your return was not only expected, but somehow natural and inevitable.

Transition is what occurs when you 'pass the body'. 'Passing the body' is termed death or dying, in your Western world, and in that, infers an end. Death that is the 'passing of the body' is an end to life in the body, the end to the exploration of dimensional life, as a body consciousness. It must be recognized that it is also the end for another important aspect of human life, and that is the human mind.

The mind, heart-mind, and body are all involved in the passing of the body consciousness and awareness, as death, as the end. And as death approaches, it is spoken of as the final days, final hours, and final moments. Finality, the end and death are for you the leaving of your Earth, the place you understand as home, as where you belong, and as where you live.

You have all of this understanding through association. Association is 'identifying with'. And for you, identifying with creates in you your sense of belonging. Many of your associations were given to you from birth. And at birth some were handed to you by your soul.

They are referred to in a non-Western understanding as your karmic connections. They are associations journeyed through time that are allowing each of you to explore and experience yourself and life. This connectedness, called karma, is a process of evolving balance and harmony. It is a major key to your ability to springboard into what is called the Journey Home.

The other aspect of this karmic connectedness is what is called Permission and Allowance. They are Divine understandings held within the center of your soul. They enable you, as human, to demonstrate compassion and forgiveness towards yourself and all

You are first, and foremost, the Breath

others in every understanding you have ever, or will ever, develop about human life and all Life. These Divine understandings are applied to your perceptions. Your 'truth', it is sometimes spoken. This is the expression and experience of yourself at the level of your human consciousness, and these perceptions allow you to hold onto and—from there—explore your life through the eyes and the actions of these 'truths'.

But many are the 'truths' you explore that are your journey, recognized and cognized as being limited and limiting. And so, they become the springboard to catapult you into other various expressions of your perceptual truths. When the body is passed, there are two factions inside you, as awareness, that want to come with you on the pass over.

On the one hand is the soul you are as a center of consciousness. It is likened to a beacon of Light signaling to you, "Come this way." It is an extraordinary center, and it holds a sense of Home for you.

When the 'energetic shell' of identity consciousness—called human body—is passed there and then you find there is another standing there as you. This is another consciousness. You find yourself as an already existing entity. It is as if you simply allowed a layer of identity, like clothing, called human body to fall away. And there you are, but draped differently now. And in that costuming, there is another identity to reacquaint yourself with. For there are no identities that are ever lost to you. They are simply removed from you, as the obvious, as *conscious awareness,* as other layers of clothing called identity are placed on top of and over other identities.

You may speak about this and view it in physical terms, as degrees of refinement or density. The human identity is one of the densest 'cloakings' or 'costumings' you will apply as an identity. Identity is really just a statement of,

> "*Oh wow! Look at me now. This is me.*"

And in each lifetime in a state of curiosity, filled with the unfamiliar and the familiar, off you go to see what life will do and be, in response and in reaction to the costuming you are. And you are curious too as to what your reactions will be to life's reactions. And so, the human *journey*, the human *life*, and the human *destiny*.

The 'passing of the body' as a conclusion to any lifetime is in response to the Call. It is not haphazard in any way. It is filled with significance. No human ego can fight the inevitability of the Call. When it is time, it is time. The longevity of a life, any life, is for a human, only as long as when the Call is sounded. In the East it is spoken of as being measured in breaths, that each lifetime has a quota of breaths. The East has a foundation of understanding that is a combination of art and science that lengthens the breath, slows the breath and spaces the breath. That aligns the breath,

You are first, and foremost, the Breath

purifies the breath, and upholds the breath as the Key to Life.

Not the simple holding onto a life, but the Key to expanding the awareness of Life. All Life rides within the breath, as awareness. Your awareness of life on Earth begins with the first breath and departs, as experiential, with the last breath. But the breath that is human is not the only breath. All Life lives as breath. And breath does not depart from you as essential to life when you 'pass the body'. Indeed, the breath continues: more refined, not oxygenated, and carried as air and wind as on your Earth, but indeed it is nonetheless a wind. It is the Wind of Life Itself, the Wind of God, the Breath of Life, and the Movement of Spirit.

All layers of identity possess a sense of breath and therefore,

> "I am a life, and as awareness, I am ongoing."

None of this will change. The human body-mind identity falls away though and is replaced by more subtle experiences and expressions of self.

You are now at a point in destiny for your Earth when such Divine understandings can reach you and assist you in opening to the notion of identity ongoing and as Life ongoing. There is yet another spectacle to consider concerning passing over, and your awakening. Awakening refers to, amongst other things, the becoming aware of 'self' as different layers of identity and Life expression. Your differently layered 'identity' allows you unique experiences and therefore understandings of Life within the different dimensions of Life and beyond those dimensions as well.

To 'pass the body' through any specific portal, gateway, or doorway allows you entry into different experiences of yourself as multi-layered Life. It is not the only way to have such an experience. In fact, 'passing the body' is the least powerful way to do it, because at the point of 'passing the body' you have run out of options and alternatives. You have, in that, also run out of time. And time is important to you as a window of opportunity to maximize your experiences and your awareness. To maximize is to gain expanded awareness of the multi-layered expression of Life and, therefore, the possibility for you to explore this as a focus of your life. To begin to know the 'you' that lives naturally, as Life, at all levels of existence.

You may say that surely the purpose of being in the body human is to experience human, third-dimensional life, as expressed on your Earth plane. And that is correct. But the degree to which you can experience life is affected by your ability to be open to feeling the exchange between you and Life, as inter-connectedness. To experience it with a focused attention that knows it is present as 'I am'.

For so many, the attention is so cluttered that the thought to even become present does not even make it

You are first, and foremost, the Breath

through to the place called conscious realization. So, there is a need for a methodology of approach and behaviour that will pull from you the powers, the desire, and the abilities to *become* present, and to *be* present.

The Eastern traditions—that more and more are finding their way into the hearts and minds of Westernized humanity—speak of an ageless body of Wisdom in which there exists the accommodations of the 'how to' and the 'why to', that will through diligence become a part of human identity and human understanding. This as a practice will, in time, open you as ever-expanding awareness, that is itself the very liberation you are seeking.

This Wisdom, as art and science, is all built upon a foundation of the Breath. It is known through experience, written of and spoken of, by many Masters who have engineered, as brilliance, their own liberation.

That refined power, that grace-filled ability to utilize the Breath to move freely through multiple realms of Life, knowing that the one constant is that the Breath Divine and the breath human are all the same lineage. It is the one continuum. It is the escalator that allows you to move from one level to the next, and back again.

You are, as human, first and foremost the Breath. All else is built from there. All else lives as result of that. All awareness exists within it. All Life exists because of it. The breath of the human flows upon an ocean that is the Breath Divine. You cannot walk away from the Breath. You will only find yourself relinquishing one to imbibe another. This is the brilliance you are, even when you are unaware of it.

To 'pass the body' — as an action of inevitability — can be re-evaluated as timing when the Breath is embraced as the 'vehicle for longevity'. Longevity is a blessing; you may grant yourself in your determination to 'pass the body' as one who allows and knows of its timing. One for whom death is not an end, but a practiced for moment that speaks,

> *"I am ongoing Life. I am a continuation. I know that within the Breath I move to where I move. I am prepared. I am ready. I am involved."*

In the moment of passing, such a one is not struck down by death. It did not 'happen' to that one. It is simply another step that is taken in the Walk of Life. It is simply another breath that is breathed, that reveals to that one their love of Life. It is another moment in which to live as witness, as testimony, to the brilliance that is the Journey of Life.

All movement that is Journey will continue on and on into the Stillness, in which all movement resides. You will continue to expand as movement. And you will continue to be the Watcher of this movement, as the one who resides as the Stillness.

The breath you are is the breath of movement, and it is

You are first, and foremost, the Breath

the breath as Stillness.

The Breath will open you to greater Movement, to greater Stillness, on and on and on.

I love you.

So be it.

Harmonizing viewpoint and view

My Beloved One,

It happens many times in a human's life that extraordinary events come knocking on your door; events that have the capacity to change your viewpoint of the world.

One's viewpoint of the world is normally changed through experience. And these experiences can take the appearance of being set in motion outside of you, in a place that is a long way away from you. And the journey of that, somehow along the way, entered into your personal world and passed on through.

Such circumstances cannot always be relied upon to present you with the understanding of how it came by you, and how you came by it. Your world has in no way prepared the Western mind to look for the step-by-step approaching of what — in the 'everything now' of the Western mind — seems to be a shock, or at least a lack of preparedness.

"I don't believe this is happening or has happened!"

This is the remark of the human who did not understand the Calling. For you, in your world, all perceptions of life bring to you their own Calling. All beliefs about life will bring to you a Calling. What is called for is always inherent in any perception, in any belief, in any attitude. The Calling is the exchange you live within as Life. Life is an exchange. Life demands that what is put out must be given back. What leaves from you must be given to. The exchange is personal. But because certain attitudes and beliefs are societal, cultural, and national, there are those exchanges that are numerically powerful. Such exchanges are ones that affect whole populations, whole nations, and your whole world.

The blindness that is the inability to see what has come—is coming—is not a blindness called lack of *ability*, it is a blindness called lack of *intent*. Intent is the choice made that speaks, "I am willing."

And the "I am willing", is backed up by the power of the mind, the power of the emotions, the power of the body ... and for others there is also the power of Spirit. When all of this is brought to bear, as focus, then there is nothing that, in time, could not become obvious.

What is obvious to one person and not another is the presence of your 'self' in the process just described. Even though it is a familiar process, tried and true in your world. It is used every day, consciously and subconsciously. So how is it then that a successful process—familiar to all humanity—is not seen within your own lives as the coming of what arrives? The inevitability of any event's arrival as a 'must occur' is because the exchange, as power, is an act of Love.

Harmonizing viewpoint and view

You question this because your world barely cognizes the interplay of your inner life and the outer life you live within.

As a Universal Truth it is spoken that one's viewpoint becomes one's view. Blame, as an occupational hazard of being human, can only be so, whilst viewpoint and view are not accepted as being centered within you. The difficulty for a humanity, long left out in the cold, in a world that has forsaken such Wisdom, means that where you *have* to begin is where you do not *want* to begin. Because to begin anywhere in the proximity of where you are currently standing is itself your greatest challenge.

To want to begin in a garden filled with beauty is an understandable choice. But there is the need right now, to at least take a good look at your own viewpoint and view and see whether this has resulted in a beautiful garden or not. It is, of course, no surprise that your own world, although having moments and times when the vision and the viewpoint together create the beautiful garden, is largely something altogether different.

The incredible ability of any human to weather the imperfections of human life is well understood by you. But the weather, like all life before you, is commonly seen as something that needs a certain preparedness. It constantly demands you adjust, as a way of being in it. The weather and your own world are not very different for you. And in their similarities, there is for each of you your personal, "This is how I deal with it."

The more you contemplate this analogy the more you will be amazed at what you can discover about yourself. There is, of course, no need to be alarmed. But look on it with a degree of excitement, for within it you will understand more about your own viewpoints and the view that is your world.

How many times do you as human ask, "Why me?"

This is the most profound question you could ask, if it was that you were truly seeking the understanding, rather than the simple expression of exasperation. To stand, in that moment, upon that threshold, when the door that is closed could be opened. And if exasperation was not the simple expletive, that of itself, is called sufficient in order that you may once again journey life awaiting the next,

"I don't believe this is happening to me."

The journey of life, that is the exchange between the within and the without, is to give you everything you say life is. Life is your greatest lover. Its only purpose is to give you everything that you say life is. The most difficult thing for many humans is to appreciate that your personal exchange with life is both that powerful and that intimate.

The human consciousness does not readily understand intimacy, for it is believed to be something that must be worked *for* and worked *at*. Intimacy speaks of your human opening up and being more

Harmonizing viewpoint and view

available. It is spoken of, as those moments when, what is kept hidden or private, is revealed. Whether it be the body, mind or soul. Intimacy is both longed for *and* feared. And this struggle is really a struggle about love. It is not about the view so much as the conglomeration of viewpoints within that creates the confusing and dissatisfying view.

The normal human focus, which is to manipulate your life to change the view, in no way alters the fractured viewpoints that are its life. You cannot hope to address your view, with intent to change it, without looking at your own assorted viewpoints that are you. The struggle in your 'world view' is the same struggle that is going on inside you with the multiple inconsistencies of a myriad of viewpoints.

And even if you become the human power that changes the view, you will only create another version of it, if nothing is done to alter the viewpoint. Blame has become the opportunity you have to not look at the interconnectedness of viewpoint and view. You have an amazing capacity to confront, as a human. Blame uses this capacity to confront the view. But the wholeness of that capacity is to be open to both viewpoint *and* view. Confrontation, that is the blame, is an action of despising. To confront—that is, the willingness to access the viewpoints—is an action of love. It is to speak of the willingness to become whole, the willingness to recognize the interrelationship between the within *and* the without of you.

THE WRITINGS

You must be amazed when reviewing the consideration that Love, that is Life, is immediately responsive to you as viewpoint. Life does not place any requirement or value on Intimacy. Your viewpoint as a 'light' or a 'darkness' is intimately understood by Life. And without judgment is willing to provide you with the vision, with the opportunity, to live your life as that expression of viewpoint. The 'demons' you perceive as your view of the world are the disowned demons that stalk the darkened corridors of your unconscious, subconscious, and conscious mind.

Your life is a signature that you place, as acknowledgement, beneath the list of your viewpoints. Many of your viewpoints are known to you. Others are less known, and others not acknowledged at all. Perversity, cruelty, and abuse can only exist in your world whilst the denial of the interconnectedness of viewpoint and view continues. For any monstrous act in your world can only have a life in the space you provide for it through viewpoint. Viewpoint that is personal, all the way through, and including viewpoint that is representative of the majority of humanity.

The acceptance of your human nature is the acceptance of no relationship between viewpoint and view. Human nature that speaks of not understanding, of not believing, of not seeing, is only possible whilst viewpoint and view are not acknowledged as one and the same. You cannot have

Harmonizing viewpoint and view

lasting peace in a world when its people will not make peace within themselves between viewpoint and view.

But you are ready now, readier than you have ever been to confront the enormity of the view. The power of the view to affect you has never been so great. And it will intensify still further. And the intensity will bring to light your powerful viewpoints. And you will begin to understand the power of the view in helping you and supporting you to translate your viewpoints.

You will begin to understand that there is a whole range of viewpoints that you have been fed, educated with, and conditioned into believing. And then there are others who have insinuated into the core of your very soul. And these are the powers that are seeking you. Dark they may be, but arms of compassion are what they seek to lie within. That they live within you, speaks of it being you that must indeed be the compassionate one.

It can be said that certain viewpoints are placed upon you from birth, as your conditioning. Others are karmic in nature and came with you, as soul human, into this lifetime. The viewpoints that are karmic, as a negative, are those that are called 'demons'.

They are the unresolved viewpoints of soul journey that still exists within you as blame, as judgment. And these 'demons', as a fixture of your life, are the unresolved love-hate that motivates viewpoint and view. The love-hate that is directed towards anything that is viewed is simply the love-hate that is contained within your own viewpoint.

Your inability or lack of desire to become intimate with your world is indeed the inability and lack of desire to become intimate with your own viewpoints as yourself. Intimacy is not the simple knowing of their existence, but the willingness to journey into any single viewpoint to the place in you where it sits as pain and suffering. To live in the righteousness of any viewpoint is no different to living in the right to destroy life. For righteousness speaks,

"I am God. I have the right to take life."

To take life without the ability to return that life is not then, the "I am God". It is the 'demon of destruction' that wants what it wants regardless of the expense or the cost. All destruction carries a price. All destruction allowed requires life to be given back.

This principle of harmonizing all life's movements, all life's exchanges, is indeed a central aspect of what is little understood as karma. To deny karma as a religious or spiritual philosophy is regulated from within the human mind by conditioning. Karma sensed as a Principle of Life, held within the soul, is a different issue entirely. At the level of soul — karma that is the viewpoint and view in human life — is well understood. But in each lifetime, the *soulular* imprint must also contend with the mind that is the cultural and conditioned imprint.

Harmonizing viewpoint and view

To whichever imprint you lean — as conscious belief — in no way alters the movement of life that is the constant actioning in your world of the opportunity to harmonize viewpoint and view. This can only be done in the willingness to love and the openness to be loved. For it is in love that compassion will, at some point, be known as self-love. And self-love will be known as the journey that results in the harmonizing, through compassion, the viewpoint and view.

Self will begin to be understood as both viewpoint and view. And in that, self-responsibility will be understood as the harmonizing, as peace: both viewpoint and view. And in acceptance of this, humanity will truly know that to live within and breathe the viewpoint that is love, the viewpoint that is happiness and joy, of compassion and peace, then that will be the vision that is your world and all life.

I love you.

So be it.

The most influential power in your life

My Beloved One,

To be chosen is to choose *yourself*. To be a chosen-one is to be one who steps forth with a clear intent. Such a one, in any field of endeavor in your world, is one who uses a remarkable degree of personal insight into the placement of themselves within their dreams. For all chosen-one's in your world, already dreamt the dream of being there. The dream to be where you are in your life is a chosen dream, picked from the many possibilities laid out before you.

What you walked towards, and into, was a dream you dreamt as possibility for you. And that possibility was filled with all kinds of experiences you wanted to explore. To taste any experience in life is the opportunity you grant yourself by choosing. Many are the choices made that you say you later regretted making. Some are the choices you made that you take no credit for making. Others are the choices you made, that you accept as such, but do not understand why.

Choices there are, and destiny there is.

To want what you want, as human, is not always the same as wanting what you want as self, as 'I', beyond human. Conflict can, and does, arise often in the heart and mind of a human, between what is chosen and what is destiny. For destiny speaks that there is an already laid-out vision *for* you, *of* you, *by* you, of your life. Destiny speaks of 'you' as soul that consciously gathered with others to discuss the purposeful evolution of your life path. Such a discussion, let us say, had input from you and others—significant others—ones whose interest in you is singular and total. They themselves are representatives of even more profound and significant others, whose interest in you is singular and total.

And all of this was designed through Divine purpose—as Divine Self—that recognized the necessity of leading you gently, and slowly but surely, as a Divine One that has chosen to experience the many, as diversity, and then return you, fully aware, to the original state of Self.

Your life is a living testimony to the Self who is witness, and to you as the journey to understand where you are upon your path of experience, as the many. At the same time, as awakening, to acknowledge where you are as awareness upon your path of Return, as the One. All of it is consciousness, is awareness. All of it is Life that is the 'Felt'.

And in your world, what is felt is explained away in thoughts that become words. Even when thoughts do not know how to explain the feeling, try it will, and try it must. For it is an indelible part of the journey to

The most influential power in your life

cognize life as felt and as thought. For you as human all life is the manifestation of both.

For you as human there is an 'out-of-step' between the *felt* and the *thought*. This is the result of an interesting state that occurs within the nature of being human, and the beginning stage of assuming consciousness in your dimensional world of Earth.

You have come from within a state of Divine Essence in which you were bathed in, and were bathing in, a sublime energy, a profound Light, the energy of which was pure Love, pure Feeling.

In an Eastern understanding, that was once a universal understanding, there is a cycle of life for each of you as human — called birth or beginning — that called forth journey in life, as life, that when completed brought change as consciousness, that you term death. Whether you understand that cycle of life as a single cycle or an ongoing spiral will, to some extent, depend on your understanding of the soul. For the soul is the focal point through which all experiences of life desired by the Divine One, journeying as the many, are transmitted to you as human self. And all your journeys as life are completed, or not, for the Divine One you are.

The soul is the house in which all past, present, and future journeys are focused. It is the middle ground occupied by yourself as human and occupied by your Self, as Divine. It is the sorting house. So, the energy of the soul has both a human aspect and a Divine aspect, a lower casing and an upper casing. The soul must direct you as human down pathways chosen by your Self Divine.

Such a responsibility is great. Such an opportunity given is not always an opportunity taken by yourself as human. The soul is the representative and is therefore aligned to the giver of opportunity. You as human are aligned to opportunity given, but you are also faced with the choice to take up the opportunity or not. What you do with the opportunity, if you do not accept it, is open to options and preferences.

Enter now the human mind. The human mind is not necessarily the creation of the soul. Where you begin your life — as circumstance — and what you draw to yourself — as circumstance — is the soul's doing. For it holds within it the energies you are as karmic human journey. As human, journeying diversity, you hold many different energies. Some of these are held in appreciation as love, and some are held in misgiving. Some are held in confusion, some are held in wonder, and some are so hot they can hardly be held at all, but hold on the soul does ... and will.

The human mind, empty at the beginning as newborn, clean and clear at birth, becomes filled in journey. And the filling is the acquired understandings of journey, the journeys of others, the journeys of a nation, the journeys of a race or caste or culture, and the journeys of a religious tradition, the

The most influential power in your life

journeys of an economic experiment, the journeys of a political experiment, and finally the journeys of relationship experiments. With so much input from outside of you it becomes clear and understandable that the mind would become a place of great confusion and contradiction.

And to this, the influence of the soul must be added as well. For remember, the soul is the communicator of your destiny. It holds the keys to your evolutionary journey along your own personal life path. The soul must be heard. But the mind controls the airwaves. The *mind* speaks,

> *"I am the collector of data about life and journey here. I am the authority. It is me you should be listening to and paying attention to."*

So, life becomes the journey of a path misunderstood. Life propelled and discerned by the human mind may not be the same as life discerned by the soul. It is important to understand that the power of the mind is gained and held by its immediacy to any life experience. The mind is loud, aggressive, passive or active, and willing to say anything that will win for it your attention.

The mind then is unscrupulous and amoral. It will use any and all means possible to maintain itself as the controlling influence over you, as consciousness, over you as awareness, as life, as a life. It needs to use this approach because it is truly only human in that manifestation. And it knows that. It is up against another influence that is far more powerful, far more significant.

The soul will not, and does not, compete with the human mind. It is sublime and undisturbed in the presence of the antics of the human mind. It does not live upon your Earth, as does your human mind. It lives in a state of *no-Time,* and as such is ultimately patient in your understanding. Its approach is wedded to the God that created it. And as such, will determine with insightful Love where best it can insert your destiny amidst the teeming possibilities presented by your human mind.

I speak to you now of the human mind that is unruly and uncontrolled. Even when your life can project great organization, great focus, great restraint, the mind can — and mostly does — run wild and unstoppable. The mind can be altered, it can be slowed, it can be seduced, it can be reckoned with, and it is capable of carrying the flag of allegiance to your soul's destiny, never totally, and never entirely ... but enough.

The mind can be trained to focus. It can be influenced by those energies greater than it. It can be introduced to that which it is as greater, as the mind of Truth, as the mind of your True Nature, as the mind of Divinity, the mind of peace, the mind of tolerance and forgiveness, and the mind of openness and acceptance. This is the mind of the One.

The most influential power in your life

And in that, the human mind is possessed by a Consciousness that is greater. So, your identity changes as perspective, as orientation, and as self-importance. Your identity as 'I am' awareness is transmuted from the Pandora's Box of perception, into a simple and profound cognizing of the Truth. Cognizing Truth speaks,

"*I am the Truth, inseparable and without distinction.*"

So, the identity held onto called human mind, human personality, and human world, is accepted for what it is. And what it is may be understood more and more clearly as you journey your path of Return. More is known, more is explained, and more is accepted.

The soul as self, in such a scenario, begins to purify that which is its human aspect and disseminate that purity into the Divine one, as Self, through the Divine aspect of the soul. And what was called journey human, takes on the Truth, and Truth becomes you as Divine awareness whilst still you walk in the body human. And in that, soul journey is propelled into more and more, greater and greater, in the ever-expanding without beginning, without end. Absolute.

The soul is the key you are looking for. When you understand its nature and its purpose you will begin to see more clearly how it is working with you in your daily lives. The soul is the most influential power within your human life for a very long time. To begin to love that which you are as soul is to begin to seek approval for your life. For amidst the mayhem or certainty you hold onto, as your existing life, inserted there in the middle of it will be your soul's destiny. Your life will be filled with your soul's intent. It will be surrounded by your soul's influence.

Your soul's most significant purpose is to be the state, in which you as human and you as Divine, stand together. It is characterized in many ways, but most significant is the soul's ability to hold both judgment and non-judgment: the human that judges and Divinity that is without judgment. A human brings to its soul its judgments. And Divinity brings to its soul its non-judgment. Since the soul is the creation of its Divinity, as created, it acts as a gateway of Truth. It speaks of the one Life. It speaks of the preciousness of that one Life and the sacredness of that one Life. It speaks about what it is *as* Life. It speaks of Love. And as Love, it knows happiness and joy, compassion and peace. All of this is your True Nature.

All that is denser in nature, your Divinity knows it only at the level of the human soul, as judged life. And at that level of understanding, it knows it is but a perception held within a dream carried in the mind of ignorance. The dreams are allowed, the perceptions are honored, and the knowing is held to.

The call to incorporate, the call to join, the call to Return is always being whispered to you from the other side of your Womb of Life, in which you are held in the Waters of Ignorance. The call is always the same.

The most influential power in your life

It is always Love calling, calling, calling to you. Gentle sweetness that is encouraging you to come from this Womb and allow yourself to be reborn into the Life of Light in which Love bathes you in its glow and its warmth. Where, like a child, you may remain in the state of Conscious Innocence, a state that knows only the beauty of all Life.

You have reached into your 'dream of separateness,' and as Divinity, succumbed as consciousness to the brilliance and incredibleness that is the illusion of the many. You know that the finding of Self in this illusion was only possible in the undoing of what was so painfully obvious. That separateness and aloneness, as aspects of the many when viewed through a vision of Love, birthed the excitement to share, and birthed the desire to give and to receive. Birthed the desire to include and become a part of. Birthed the feeling that all could be *One* and yet be the *Many*.

That is what lives as Self in the center of the Heart of Love. In this state, Divine meets human, human meets Divine. And the soul rejoices, and in the celebration of Life, merges with its Maker.

I love you.

So be it.

Life, as the Mother

My Beloved One,

There are many opportunities to view the workings of the Blessed Mother, sometimes referred to as the Goddess. The many faces of the Divine Mother have captured the hearts and minds of many humans throughout the ages. Rare it is, that anyone has been able to capture that essence as pure Self.

The interesting thing about such exploits and experiences is that the focus has not always been on the core of the manifestation, but on its outer and outward expressions. The difficulty for humanity is that when dealing with the Mother, they do not understand Her True Nature. It does not matter whether you live in the body woman or the body man, the same lack of understanding exists. It does not matter that a woman feels herself to be more accurately the embodiment of this Divine principle. It does not matter that a woman moves, as life, through configurations of this principle. It matters not who, as gender, can claim ownership of the Mother as True Nature, for She lives, as Life, within All.

The fascination with the Goddess in Western culture is more a fascination with stimulation. For the Goddess motivates life through stimulation. She is the bearer of all stimulation, and so it is easy to be drawn into the feminine principle at this level of interaction. Ease, in this case, represents what is natural.

The stimulation factor is more the doorway—the portal—through which you enter into life, and you enter into the Mother. It is profoundness beyond all words, and it is a simplicity that allows it to be called ordinary. You cannot allow yourself to be fooled into believing that you have captured the essential Mother, simply because you have become captivated by Her ability to stimulate. Whether you exist, as the witness, to such stimulation in others, or you are the experience of such stimulation, as both, you are only touching the tip of the iceberg that is the Goddess, that is the Mother Divine.

You say that the Goddess is tangible, in that she is embodied in the female shape. That she is embodied in the female psyche. That she is embodied in the female genitals. That she is embodied in the female beauty is all true to a point. It is, however, only a costume that is worn. It is a design that has its purpose and function. It is a creation that allows for what is pure to flow.

Flow is movement; the movement is energy that is life force. Life force is that which holds all Life, as present. It holds life in Time, as past and future. And it holds all Life that has its existence beyond and outside of Time. You cannot capture life force. You cannot

Life, as the Mother

capture the Goddess. Any attempt to capture Her and hold onto Her, to hold Her separated, as if in a vessel of some description, will immediately leave you dealing with an apparition, an illusion, of what you believe you had and have. The Mother is the Flow. Flow is the essence of the Mother principle. This Nature allows for, and is the precursor and energizer of, all Flow.

Any ritual that uses any artifacts, of any description believed to be an expression of Her Embodiment are, as a vessel, lifeless and empty of the great Power as movement and flow. Certainly, the human mind, the human body, the human emotions, can be stimulated by being in the presence of such artifacts. But that stimulation is of itself meaningless to the overall understanding, as awareness, of the great Mother as the One Goddess, that is the feminine principle of Light and Life, of the One.

The powerlessness I speak of is the powerlessness that is within the human psyche that can only conceive of powerless rituals in order to invoke the Divine. Emptiness, that is the lack of presence of the Goddess, must be hidden, must be veiled. So ritual is called upon to invoke stimulation, and in stimulation the Mother is vowed to be present. The Mother is always present, with or without the implications of any rituals, simple or complex. The Mother has no need to preserve Her identity or channel Her essence through the limitations of any ritual. Long before there was any humanistic ritual—the Divine Father—the most precious Divine Mother created the most profound play of interconnectedness that would cause the Father—that would create for the Mother—the most incredible dance of expansion on and on forever.

You cannot imagine, in your human mind, the absolute enormity of this dance. The arrow of intent moving forever inwards, forever outwards. And within the arrow of intent lays the Womb of Realization in which all Life is a Being-ness and a Becoming. All Life is a forever-ness, realms within realms, planes within planes, dimensions within dimensions, planes within dimensions, onwards and onwards, inwards and inwards as the Forever-ness.

Human play, that is ritualistic, is more a representation of fascination than anything else. For a human must, at some point, step back from its own creation in order to own what it truly is. To call to the Mother, as a human, is to call into the Mother only as far as your human soul can reach. And the soul, in its human aspect, cannot take any human into the Mother, as the Goddess, as the embodiment of Creator Power.

To live as human, surrounded by the created, is to spend time and energy building mementos. And mementos are more a remembrance of what has gone before, of what is lost. They are a tool of remembrance. But remembrance, for a human, is more a movement to capture and hold onto a memory, and in the

Life, as the Mother

memory the feelings for what has gone. But memory that is human, is itself captured and held by Time. And Time that is of your world cannot be either the gateway, or your means of travel, to reconnect you with Self, as essence, as Mother, as Goddess. It can only avail you of Her trappings, Her finery, Her bejeweled-ness, Her beauty, as it is seen by you. All of this, as stimulation, is human you, human world, human vision, human perception, and human understanding.

To appreciate this, at this level of understanding, is to give back to the Mother her freedom. Not that you, on one level, could ever take from Her, flow and movement. You can, however, as human mind, isolate. And to isolate the Mother from Life and hold Her captive in rituals perceived by human minds, to uphold the human heart, is to deny the very flow that the ritual is said to preserve and call forth. All that is called forth is stimulation, of body and mind and heart. To create anything more is to bow down at the feet of the One, as Goddess who is being called and surrender to Her movement within you.

To control or be controlled is the mind of the human, is the heart of the human, and is the world of the human. Any simple humanistic ritual is still about control and being controlled, to lead or be led. To be the light or the one who seeks the light.

All of this can be a game, a great fantasy to attract the attention of a human towards a life that is not an obvious display of pain, separation and 'lostness'. The ritual is the stimulation of the senses that can lift your being out of the state of feeling trapped and helpless. The great Mother, to one who is feeling trapped and helpless, must Herself be captured. So that She may become the elixir that will obliterate, at least for a time, the obviousness of the human condition, of the human dilemma.

To use the Goddess in this way simply becomes the play of human design that speaks to invite the Mother to the world called human control. That world is a clogged and cluttered world, filled with all kinds of configurations that come into effect to maintain control. This is a channel that restricts movement and flow, and therefore, inhibits the appearance of the Mother Goddess.

To join with the Mother, the Goddess, beyond your world of stimulation and the rituals they provoke is to surrender to the Goddess. To be willing to surrender to Life as it is. To be willing to surrender to Life as you are. To be ready to surrender to the relationship you are, that is your life, unfettered with camouflaging rituals that seek to portray life as pretty, as beautiful, as sweet, as gorgeous, as heavenly, as pure. Life that is this, that is a projection of your own mind and heart's intent, is not life at all that the Mother can truly live within as Her purity.

It is not Life that is Flow. It is life that is captured in a moment and the moment itself is called 'my life'. And

Life, as the Mother

you breathe into that moment over and over and over again until you become satisfied that the illusion can exist as reality, for you. And now you can comfortably, confidently, call it 'my life' and then set about filling it with the furniture that is the enhancement of it as reality. Such a sidestepping of Life is a sidestepping of the Mother in Her purity. It is a sidestepping of what can truly be yours in this lifetime. For you live now in a world whose time it is to be more at the effect of the Goddess, as the feminine principle. Whether you be a man or woman matters not. For within you, you will be motivated and moved in your experience of life governed and defined by this principle.

It is a wondrous time to play, for Her energies of flow and movement will allow for so much life that once seemed undefined and ungoverned. But to live in the juices of Her sweet flow does not always bring you to the State of Being, called, "I am Mother. I am Goddess."

To journey that Path is to relinquish all understandings, all appreciations for what you say you already know. For the Mother as Goddess is a wild ride, and control will not allow you to stay the course. You have before you, as a path of possibility, an enduring relationship with the Goddess that will first call on you to hold the Mother's hand, whilst She leads you to where She already lives within you, as 'You'. For the Mother who has spawned all Life, never judges any child from Her Womb. You are filled with

Her offspring. Your life is that creation.

The Mysteriousness that is invoked by the Mother is really only the unexplored reaches of Life that you — as the human who is in control — will not allow yourself to explore. The great mechanism of Allowance, the movement through doorway after doorway is what is called the mysteriousness of the Mother. No amount of ritual will ever create an opening of any doorway, unless the one that stands at the doorway is themself *already* the doorway.

The human mind, as a veil, does not recognize the doorway or know if it is, as human, itself the doorway. The human mind is the distraction that speaks,

> *"There is no doorway and there is no 'you' that is standing at the doorway, as that doorway."*

The mind of denial wants to give you its lifeless version of Life called, "Let me design and imprint this ritual called, 'You want a doorway?' I will create a doorway for you."

As such it becomes life imitating Life, the ego human imitating the Mother, ritual imitating Initiation, the student imitating the Master, and ignorance imitating Knowing. All of this is a circle and although it could be called entertaining, it is however, not enlightening.

To flow, as the Mother, is to experience the movement of your own life as a river flowing towards the great ocean. You cannot call your river the ocean, just as you cannot call your puddle a creek. You can only explore

Life, as the Mother

what you are. If you are the puddle, explore that. If you are the river, explore that. And when you merge with the ocean you will explore that too.

Each of you has your own stream of consciousness. Each of you has your own perspectives. Life, as the Mother, demands that such perspectives reflect the Truth of Her glory. For you as human, this is your greatest challenge and your single greatest quest.

I love you.

So be it.

Your world, constructed and performed

My Beloved One,

You have felt *so* corrected many times in your life, in such a way, that you grew to have enormous doubt concerning your ability to know anything about what you were doing with your life, as your life. You began to dispute, in your heart and mind, your existence as intelligence. All of this did not last consciously at the forefront of your attention, but it did last, and has lasted in that place inside you, in which you evaluate yourself. Where you approach others and are approached by others. In the arena of interaction with others, this dominates. It is what lies hidden in all your exchanges.

No matter the sweetness, the niceness, the informality or the powerfulness, all of it is a coating that surrounds you as your public persona, as a one '*of* the world and *in* the world'. You have needed to find a way to grant yourself a form of composure, where you can function in a world that wants to give to you, and you to it.

It is not a time to tear anything down, but to simply become aware of what you are performing. And what underlies your performances. The belief that you can gain something from this performance has already been proven by you, and in that, has become solidified. You have always been looking to make solid and substantial the belief that what you perform is really you. Performance for you comes from within the heart and mind of confusion. It becomes the constant exercising of doubt that wants to give you something in exchange for what has gone away.

What has gone away is you, as Source, you as awareness that is a simple openness to all and everything. That Source is looking for nothing and therefore can truly see all. Not just what your mind tells you is there, but more, much more. The mind of such a one is itself the Mind of Openness that you may call Spirit, you may call it Everlasting Life. For there is Life to behold that is Everlasting. It is not a life constructed by your human mind and heart, but it can view what your heart and mind has constructed for you. It views it as love looking for Love. It views it as life lived outside of being Love. It is life seeking to know, consciously *and* unconsciously. It is life constructed and performed, living outside of the certainty of, "I know who I am".

To speak from within the constructed and performed, that you know who you are, is really to say you know what you *are not*.

"I am not Life Everlasting.

I am not God.

I am not my Father, my most Divine Mother.

Your world, constructed and performed

I am not Love.

I am not Peace.

I am not all Knowingness."

Every time you are in any circumstance where you find yourself having to uphold what you have constructed, as yourself, then you are indeed denying the Truth of who you truly are. This duality exists within you, unresolved. For many, for most, resolution has become the intention to have your life move in a certain way. Life and you attempting to work it out together. You and life locked into some kind of struggle in which you are doing your best to make it all work.

The perception of struggle has been constructed by you in your performance of life. Struggle holds, as glue, your constructed, performing world together. Such a world is not the true world you have around you. It is only what you have come to understand, and it is your understandings that are holding it in place. For someone who is not holding their world in this place, then in that Freedom for however long it lasts, they can see at those times, what they are doing as their human constructed nature. They can easily see and know of its reactive-ness to everything, and everything to it.

At the same time, they are also existing within the realm of Consciousness called, 'nothing has changed'. There is a state called, 'nothing has changed' and you still live there, *in* that state, *as* that state, but you do not consciously experience it any more, or at least, very little. The expansiveness of your sensory preoccupation is so complete that it easily smothers your awareness and your willingness to be aware of the Unchangeable One you are.

So, it has simply become a foregone conclusion that this 'You' can be doubted as existing at all. In denying its existence you trap yourself in the inconclusive quest of constantly wanting to know, "Who am I?"

Your human mind wants that answer. Your human heart wants that answer. Or so they say. The truth is they *do not*. The longing to know comes from a deeper place than the mind and heart you have constructed.

It is the calling from your human soul to the Divine One you are, wanting explanation for all that you find yourself in as life human. Life for you is not easily explainable or understood when you know yourself to be different from it.

When difference is not clearly understood, and therefore cannot truly be explained, it cannot succumb to your mind and heart's evaluation. And just as well, because this is the arena of doubt you live in as consciousness, and here you will not accept Truth easily. You may entertain it, both mentally and emotionally, but to actually have it penetrate your Being is a whole other story.

You cannot hope to realize the Self without first sitting

Your world, constructed and performed

with this conflict. You may sit with it for days, weeks, years, and lifetimes until you are prepared to feel the tingling excitation that is the Self Realized, entering you and approaching your conscious awareness. It is doing so because you are letting this happen. You are wanting this to happen. You have dropped enough of your defenses to let the, 'who am I' come to you — not to your human mind, not to your human heart, but to your human being. That which you are, simply as awareness. That which you are, first and foremost, as consciousness, before the constructed and performed molded you an identity in order for you to relate and be related to.

It will dawn on you that you, as Self Realized, relates to you as human from a state of Purity, in a state of Simplicity, in a state of Being-ness. The exchange is purely energetic, no explanation is given, and no explanation is needed. You were penetrated and you penetrated. You have merged into a state of conscious awareness called simply, "I am."

For the longest time, the after-effect of such an experience is to want to explain it, to give it meaning, to make it more rational, understandable, and believable. Even simply putting it into words, no matter how fumbling or bumbling — cute or brilliant — you will know only that it was an experience that has no real need for explanation and cannot truly be explained.

The human mind is divorced from the Mind that is

truly the Heart that is the One that is Love. This separation is the existence of the conflicted mind, the mind that is trying to make sense and explain what cannot truly be explained. Even when explanation is offered, as it is now, in these Writings, it is not that they overcome, as if with a magic wand, the overriding presence of separation. It is more that these Writings are entering into your world—which is the world of your mind—to give it something to focus on, that will allow the mind and the heart to have moments and times when it may fixate on possibilities beyond what is offered to you *from* your world, *by* your world.

It is a portal where, once entered, you may grant yourself opportunities to melt away what has been constructed and performed for so long. When you do this, you will eventually arrive at unrealized possibilities. And these possibilities become highly personal. And your journey moves more and more into true uniqueness, in which Realization has a personal taste and a personal flavor. And you are more and more entering states of Purity that cannot be even spoken of, or about.

So, in a real sense you become quieter and quieter. And you will find yourself withdrawing from this constructed and performed world. But in doing so, you will find yourself entering into deeper and greater experiences of Life, in which the innate sweetness and deliciousness can be tasted and savored. That sweet

Your world, constructed and performed

Life that was, and is, always there, but is only rarely experienced from within the state of 'constructed and performed'.

All of the great Masters who have ever shared their Self Realized state with their fellow humanity, were always in the same situation. Attempting to have you understand — even as a simple contemplation, even as the simple desire to open your heart — that to have you feel the desire to awaken yourself to the world, you are as Self Realized. All the great Teachers wanted only one thing for their beloved humanity: to let them have a taste of what it is they truly are.

To let them savor the moments of being in the presence of the Realized One. To let them feel what it is like to be known and loved. To be allowed to have themselves be just who they are, with all their perceived shortcomings and all their perceived brilliances. All of them constructed and performed so as to bury themselves in their beliefs as reality.

In the presence of the Light of Life, that is these 'Ones', you will truly sense the fragile state of each and every one of your constructions and your performances. This fragile state is not soft and supple. It is brittle and, therefore, is feared that it may break and shatter. Every individual will truly know of their own uniqueness in the presence of such a One. All of the blurred lines and fuzzy edges, all of the opaqueness disappears in the presence of such a One. All of what allows human life to wend and wind its way through the dullness that

THE WRITINGS

you accept as life in your world.

The dullness and opaqueness, the lack of clarity, is really only the presence of what is *not* Life. Such an experience is what you take for granted and accept as normal. And you are right. It is the mind and the heart of the constructed and performed that is the separation, that is the obscurity, that is the question: "Who am I?"

That the question would even be lodged is itself telling you that who you are *presently* is not who you *are*. So, in a sense, you may begin by rejecting what you are currently.

So, the, 'who am I?' is really the asking for directions as to *where* to go and *how* to go to find your Self. It also implies that in some place, some state, buried deep inside you, there is a knowing of another you. But you do not remember *who* and *what* that you is. How you felt, and what you knew.

The 'who am I?' is the crying out for direction. The 'who am I?' is the 'You' penetrating your constructed and performed world in the only way it can — as energy. The cry for assistance is the only way left for you, who is the performing one, to initially spark tingles of Realization. Such movement is always necessary as you begin your journey of awakening.

The solidness that comes through performance of the constructed must be worn away. You cannot detonate it or vaporize it. You can only wear it away. To wear it

Your world, constructed and performed

away is the purpose of any and all true spiritual paths. As a soul, you are on a life path and it is always spiritual, whether you consciously acknowledge that or not. But there comes a destiny for every soul when the life path and the spiritual path awaken to each other. This Awakening looks different for every single human, and the orchestration of destiny is unique for each one.

You cannot, and will not, be swallowed by your experience of this. Your life is your life. You have it as constructed and performed for as long as you want it. You will constantly feel in that a sense of embattlement in which you are struggling with your own call to bring forth, 'who am I?'

Any battle you have with anyone else, any unresolved differences you have with anyone else, is all your own unwillingness to take your next step that will be an answering to your call,

"Who am I?"

To not answer the call ushers forth the realization that constructed and performed still provides you with the safety called *separated*. And separated allows you to not forgive and not be forgiven. All forgiveness is about what cannot, and has not, been tolerated within your own soul, as life journey. This is not a path you can remain on forever. Denial has its own calling in each lifetime. It is death that awaits you. Coming upon you to gather you up, whilst once again you attempt to remake your world from within the chambers of unresolved self-love. That is what you are. You are Self Love. In that state you are the unquestionable and the unquestioning in which all is known, and all is felt. All is within, as Love.

So, to the Halls of Understanding the soul must attend. To gather again the momentum to tackle what is questionable and what is still being questioned. To enter again the chambers that hold constructed and performed as life. And awaiting you there is the calling from the Self Realized One you are to consider the letting go of what is still so solid and defined within you.

You are now on that doorstep. So many of humanity are ready now for the next step. Awakening is inevitable for you, in the same way that sleep was as you entered your world as a Dream of Ignorance. It cannot be known as a dream until all that makes it solid—all that you are holding onto and will not release from—is bowed to in Love, in compassion and allowance, as the Breath of Peace becomes you, in each moment you inhale, and each moment you exhale.

You *are* the Breath, and you are *within* the Breath. Inside the Breath there is awareness to be gained. In that state you will know you are Love and you are Peace. You will taste it and it will fill you for moments, minutes, or hours. And in that state, you will penetrate all those around you in that Love, that Peace, and they will feel it ... or not.

Your world, constructed and performed

Your world, at this time, offers you the greatest opportunity there has ever been to awaken into the Self Realization that is, "I know who I am."

I love you.

So be it.

The Coming of the Goddess

My Beloved One,

Everything you have ever wanted to achieve is made possible in this, and any lifetime, by your commitment to overturn all of the inbuilt sabotage, as lethargy, that invokes an otherwise amazing individual to become less than its greatest destiny.

Why does this occur so often in the lives of a humanity that is constantly focused on striving to be as successful as one possibly can?

At this time success as a word has been given a restricted and limited opening in its frame of reference. And that may be okay, because the most appreciated area of your life in which you can gain great status is in the arena of work as, 'what you do for a living'. This has been significant in determining the measure of a man for a long time now on your world, and it is in this Age becoming more a reference point for women as well. It is no longer enough to simply 'marry well' if you are a woman. That, as a measure of status and success is, increasingly so, not enough and in some arenas not of any consequence at all.

Success has always been associated with power, even

THE WRITINGS

if power did not always translate into economic and financial wealth, it has always translated as a measure of influence. Success, power, and influence when married to economics and finances create for that individual an appearance of heaven on earth. That whatever is desired can be made available, and whatever does not want to be available may be seduced into being so.

The history of Woman on this plane has never been given to you fully for fear that a particular order could be unseated as the power to control. The Nobility of Life has been overturned by this power in order to erase the possibility that the true power could come to life on this world. This power is embodied in Woman as essence. And it is not that Woman alone is this power, but that she holds a particular focus that prevents the deviation to occur. Deviations of the kind that are now so prevalent as practice in your world.

This ability to prevent certain deviations requires that Woman returns to certain understandings, certain knowings of her True Nature. For within True Nature there is the expression 'Woman' and the expression 'Man'. There is the manifestation of Goddess and the manifestation of Lord God. So, Life made manifest in this and all dimensions has, as impact, the signature of both Goddess and God. Each is to the other a co-founder, a co-creator, a co-creation of all worlds.

So, in the Heavens there is the dual magnificence of both the great Lord, and the supreme beauty, as the

The Coming of the Goddess

magnificence of the Goddess. And it cannot be declared who is greater at the level of the One, for in that state all is the *Mother Father God*. To speak as Goddess, to speak as great Lord,

> "I am more brilliant, more potent,
> more the Wisdom of the One,"

is beyond calculation, beyond the Mind of the One. For to know that, is to be that and to achieve that as 'I Am', any Lord, any Goddess, must merge completely into that which is beyond any comparison. They must merge back into the Beginning as the original and unending One as the *Mother Father*, the *Father Mother*, the *I AM*.

In your world, however, there is not the experience of this as an 'evenness', beyond comparison. There is not the simple Union that as the pure reflection of the two great powers: autonomous Goddess and autonomous Lord God.

To speak of autonomy at this level of Life, of Existence, is not the same as your understanding of autonomy. For you, the inherent sense of separateness, of dividing the whole into two halves, and then giving loyalty, power, allegiance, as opinion — as attitude — to one over the other as if you could in your human mind possibly understand what you are doing; what you are measuring; or what you are comparing.

Autonomy of God-Goddess is not about the denial of the Union, it is about the significance of aspects of the

THE WRITINGS

True Nature of each to affect and influence, to bring about a greater manifestation, a greater expression, and a greater experience of the Union. For the Union is ultimate, it is everything, so the nuances of that Union can be explored infinitely, and indeed their very existence invites the greatest Lords and the greatest Goddesses to explore that Union through these nuances infinitely. And that has brought the attention and focus of these Great Ones to your Earth, and elsewhere, where there can be fruitful experiences of these nuances.

Here on your world what is seen as fruitful is what has the possibility and potency to come to pass. And this as Life, as Creation, has the opportunity like never before to move, as power, into the lives of each and every individual consciousness in a way that has not happened before.

For it is already spoken, in mystical circles from ages ago, that a Golden Age would come to this world carried as Consciousness, more evenly balanced as power in the hands of both Lord God and Goddess. Neither would, as Union, see themselves as greater. Each would call upon the other to instigate great movement as a powerful shift in Consciousness. Both would bow to the need to invite the other as power, as nuance, to help manage and orchestrate the vast shift that was designed and prophesized to occur.

And none of this would go unnoticed by the peoples of your world, for their lives would change, and have

The Coming of the Goddess

changed. And this change is experienced as rapture and joy in the Heavens for the effect of what is occurring on your Earth plane is being felt elsewhere within all levels of Life. And, although the desire to make predictions about futures that can already be seen, there is still the blessed life of your humanity and many other expressions elsewhere that are walking into that future, one step at a time, one day at a time, one challenge, one opportunity, one success — all of them as momentum are changing Consciousness everywhere.

On your world, do not look to your media as it is the last place where you will see signs or significant alterations, particularly in the arenas of politics and economics. For it is here that the deepest levels of control and manipulation manifest in your world. For the powers that are responsible reason that control at this level of your lives guarantees them the greatest likelihood of preventing what they know is coming, as Great Change. Even amongst their own group the influence of the nuances, carried as Goddess within the Union that is both your present manifest creation and your yet-to-manifest creation is now happening.

For as mighty as the power of the mind really is, and as helpful as it has been to those who utilize it to mastermind the manifestation of their desired future, the appearance of the Goddess has added to this power of manifestation a quality of life that is not easily measured, grasped or held within the power of mind. For it is the nuance of the Goddess within all Consciousness, all Life, all Existence. It is the presence within the "I AM" Consciousness of the One of an infinite quality and power to absorb Life, and to be absorbed. So, as nuance it can take in Life, and in that experience, change it and fertilize it with another consciousness, a greater understanding, and a higher nature.

All of this, as spiritual awakening, has created the look and feel of a completely different pathway than what has been traditionally the manner for a seeker of Enlightenment to conduct themselves, and to live their lifepath. No longer the separation that is the power of the mind as the dominant influence, the nuance of the Lord God, Father Creator.

For the nuances of the Goddess were seen as all too pervasive, too all-consuming as Life, to benefit the path of the adept. It was too filled with the juice of life, the taste of exquisite creation. The complications, the temptations, the distractions were too great for the simple, but direct, power of the mind. So, in the past, isolation from the Goddess, from the delights of creation was thought to offer the aspiring pupil on the path of spiritual awakening their best opportunity to awaken.

But such a way, as a path, has not always created the results that it was hoped for, prayed for. For in this expression of The Way, the Union was altered, it was controlled. And Goddess, the great Mother within the

The Coming of the Goddess

Union, looked at what was occurring, and She too had to make a re-evaluation of The Way to awaken the Consciousness.

The inherent "left out in the cold" dynamics had to be moved beyond. The great Goddess in the Heavens had to be willing to become involved in the Play of Life within the Dimensions. She had so much as Mother to contribute — as Divine influence — that could change the look of manifested Creation. For indeed something new, as a course of action at this level of Divinity, needed to occur. Life as a creation had lost its way and had become mired in the constant push and pull of the fruits of creation, all of which as nuance carried Her power, Her essence. So, to unravel the Consciousness from this entrapment required Her involvement within and upon the path of spiritual awakening.

And so, for agreement to occur the great Lords have had to bow to the knowing that a spiritual path, as a description, would have to look and feel greatly different to what it has for thousands of years as the nuance of the Lord God and the power of the mind.

The agreement was that the Union would, as a togetherness, begin to implement a different way for spiritual awakening to occur. The significance and importance, the absolute imperativeness of the continued focus on the power of the mind, was never to be questioned. Such potency and power had already been shown as the way to awaken, but in these times Life — as Goddess, Mother — has spoken, "We must awaken all my children."

The invocations of the Goddess, as the Creation power within the nuances of Her True Nature, allowed the Union of Lord God and Goddess to birth into dimensional life powerful influences that had hitherto not been present. And so, all levels of life have begun to experience the effect of this influence. It is this influence that will carry humanity into their Golden Age. But it is not so just for your Earth plane and its people: as an Age it affects all Life everywhere. And that will cause a shift of profound magnitude, as a ripple effect in Consciousness, through all strata of dimensional existence and beyond.

So, for now you must look again within your own world and your own life to see the nuances of the Goddess at work. It will be easy for you if you put your focus on the arrival on your plane of existence of a great opening in the Consciousness that has allowed all expressions of beauty to begin to manifest as a quest to have, to indulge, to master, and to participate.

The Goddess demands, as nuance, that all Life be seen as an expression of Her extraordinary power. And that power has been tapped, and in that, the influences of your electronic and computer world, your communication and media expansion, all of it as an expression of the Goddess in partnership with the Lord God nuance of mind power.

This seduction of beauty married to mind power is

The Coming of the Goddess

everywhere present as your expanding material culture, but it is also present as observation and experience in, and for, Woman. She has never been more overtly powerful and influential in your established historical times. She has never been so overtly ambitious for herself and her world. She has never tasted the power of life here like she does now.

And it can barely be controlled by those who fear this. For there is a need by those who control everything here to channel this feeling of power into areas of your culture where it can be subjugated and diluted. Where this power can be distracted.

The purpose of those who fear the coming of this Golden Age and the Goddess, know that they must separate wherever possible, whenever possible, Woman from the nuances of her True Nature. Separate her from the knowing of and experiencing, from the Truth of the Union with the Lord God, and the power of the mind.

The nature of Goddess within Woman on this Earth is being pulled and pushed both ways in order to keep Woman un-centered. *Un-Centered* lessens the power, lessens the influence and it is hoped, in that, it will stall or completely eradicate the possible coming of this Goddess Age, the Golden Age.

So, in the Heavens, the Goddess is being asked to take on a much more active and involved role and participate with humanity more directly, bringing Her vast power—as Her particular nuances of the Union that is the One—to bear. Passing through Her great unwillingness that is the decision, as Life, to not give in to the inherent challenges that have always been agreed upon when the path of spiritual awakening is looked at for how best to give Truth and gather the results of awakening, as Consciousness.

To control a power that is within all Creation and beyond all Creation has always been the challenge. Even the Goddess as a collective, has admitted that the stretch and reach into every aspect of Creation, as Creation, makes it difficult to generate just one focus for Her nature as nuance. Since, of Her very Nature, She holds the multiple focuses of:

*"I am Goddess Mother. I am focused **on** everything, **in** everything, **as** everything."*

And the 'Lord God power of the mind' was seen as essential to the birthing of this Golden Age, for the nuance of His Nature granted Him as a Collective the ability to focus specifically.

So, the one supported the other; the one knew that it could not achieve this without the other. The Golden Age required the Union. And so too now your spiritual path requires the Union.

And the deliciousness—and the challenge—is this spiritual awakening must be birthed from within Creation within Life, within your life, your world, your work, your journey, your neighborhood, your

The Coming of the Goddess

city, your state, and your nation.

It is not within the True Nature of the Goddess to completely isolate Herself from all that She is as Creation. So, in order that it be utilized for your awakening, Her power must be grasped from within your lives in the world. There is no desire within the Goddess to seek that awakening on a secluded path. It has been done; it has been accomplished, and the fruits of that as The Way are the rich heritage of Wisdom that has been handed down through the ages to you.

A fork in the road occurred that created religious paths as a means of holding to that Wisdom. But wisdom, that is no longer alive as the living Presence of the one that is their Wisdom, can no longer embody the power demonstrated as the 'I Am' Presence of that Master. A Master whose Awakened state alters the path of the adept, or student, and who sits before them by uplifting through practices, their karmas. On the other hand, the wisdom held to—and venerated by—the 'followers' of One who has already left their body has allowed for dilution: dilution through interpretation. Dilution through perceptions that come from the human ego's desire to manage a spiritual path. This you now speak of as religion.

Religion can only have a place on your path for a certain period of time, in the big picture. You may say that there is no more you desire or aspire to than to be an upright follower of the wisdom of that religion.

THE WRITINGS

The Masters of the past who now have vast followings in their name, called religions, must now work with the arrival of the Goddess. For all that has been formulated as religious doctrine and dogma is only to create edifices and structures. Not from a desire within the original one, the living Master, but to create and fulfil human ego fantasy and the journey of that, as human life, for those who claim to be the clerics of that religion.

Such a path, although taken on in the name of the Master who originated the Wisdom, as that Wisdom, over time becomes completely dead as a way to awaken. For religion as a path is all about the Master, whereas the living Master was all about the seeker.

Only a living Master can see through the Veil, and in that, see into the soul of each of its followers, students, seekers and adepts. These ones can be initiated, each to their own level, so the path is alive, and rich, and full. They are fully engaged, fully occupied with the essence of the Master, and they will remain that way until soul conflict — as the *bump in the road* — derails the path and their focus for a day, a week, a month, a year … or a lifetime.

To be upon a path, a religious path, allows the ego human nature to be totally in control of its spiritual destiny. The ego, in any moment, has a place for it in any human's life.

And this, as an aspect of your human life, is well

documented on your world, as not a way to awaken spiritually, but to be a good human, and in that as a Child of God, gain access to a heaven, a place, a state of reward. This as a spiritual path has stalled through lack of pure Wisdom, lack of the Presence of the Living Truth that is the embodiment of everything a human thinks its religious path is about.

Alongside this religious way there has always existed the way of the Goddess, lived *as* life, *through* Life. The way of the Goddess has always been:

"I am Life before you. Venerate Me, admire Me, desire Me, contemplate Me, join with Me, walk with Me."

And the life She is, is not the life of human nature, but of Nature, of creation as everything that is before you as living life. From the greatest of the greatest as your sun, to the tiniest of the tiniest, the smallest of the small upon the land, in the Earth, within the oceans, the waters and in the wind. She, as The Way, demands and commands your admiration, your involvement, your willingness to be attracted to Her, to be enticed and titillated by Her. Such is Her way as nuance of the One.

At this time, She has moved beyond creation before you into creation within you as you, and in that *has* created, and *is* creating, a completely different platform as your spiritual path, as your spiritual awakening. It has never been done this way before and, as such, creates new possibilities upon the Earth and within the Heavens.

You must understand what this already means for you as your spiritual path and your spiritual direction. All that has already occurred within your own life, and observed in the lives of those around you, is only the beginning of what is to become a path into a future. A future that, if committed to, will bring to all life the opportunity, as choice, that invites you, and speaks to you:

> *"Let us awaken, each and every one of us. Let us move as far as we can upon our unique and individual paths into the awakening consciousness of, 'I am love'.*
>
> *I am peace. I am happiness and joy. I am compassion.*
>
> *I love all life and my life. Let me know myself as more.*
>
> *Let me reach, as steps upon my way, into deeper and deeper knowing of, 'I am this, I am that'.*
>
> *And let it be felt as 'I know'. And in 'I know' be in that a Service. And as that, let it become me as Life.*
>
> *For to serve, I already cognize, is the purpose of all Life everywhere."*

This is the Union, the way of Lord God-Goddess. It is what is upon you now and, in that, your spiritual awakening is being offered to you.

I love you.

So be it.

Ambition, the Distorter of The Wisdom

My Beloved One,

Wisdom has come in many forms throughout the ages, and what it looks like and sounds like always carries the times it was spoken, as how it was spoken.

And in whatever culture this Wisdom came forth, then the people interpreted and utilized this Wisdom as their way of life. The Vedas gave a whole continent Wisdom to create and live life by. The Buddha of the East changed the meaning of life as it was understood for millions of people throughout many cultures. And Jesus and Mohammed came to the Middle East as the Bearers of the Wisdom.

And in many other cultures the Wisdom was venerated through The Mother, The Goddess most specifically, and in times gone by — and even now — these ones as practitioners have been called Pagan.

All the same Wisdom as Life, Life here, and Life beyond, was given as understanding to a humanity who hungered to know:

"Where do I fit in? How do I fit in?"

And in great civilizations — as was the Persian, and the Greek, and before them the Egyptian — there was at the very heart of those civilizations, the Wisdom, as the centerpiece of what made that culture the brilliant expression of Life that it was. If you spend time only looking into the cultural flavor of Wisdom, then the essence can be missed. How any civilization—as culture—has utilized the Wisdom to fit and work for them *can* skew the perception of the original Purity. What a civilization has done, is doing, or will do with the Wisdom is all at the expense of political, economic, and spiritual-religious needs and desires which are truly seeded from Ambition.

The Wisdom *is* the Wisdom. What you are left with, as understanding, is how a culture utilizes it. Any civilization, as culture, will pull from the One Tree of Wisdom the fruits that best serves its ambition. Civilization only comes about because of Ambition, and the greater the ambition the greater the civilization. But greater is, as a meaning, open to different interpretations. The focus is capable of covering a broad spectrum of possible goals and outcomes as achievement. And this can be easily identified within previous great civilizations.

This similarity of all ambition is in the realm of expansion. Civilizations, as empires, are always about expansion. And in the expansion, the Wisdom, is carried into 'this place' and 'that place' and in the name of the Empire it is spoken of as 'the Wisdom'.

Even in these times the Wisdom is carried as the 'god of expansion' in the name of the 'empire' that upholds

Ambition, the Distorter of The Wisdom

it. Was this ever the purpose of the one, or ones, who originally cognized Truth and placed words upon what is pure Light and pure Sound? This was always the origin of their Teaching. Using language to identify, as closely as possible, with the purity of Truth that lives outside and beyond language. Sanskrit — an ancient language in parts of India — still uses as the written and spoken word an original pure sound language.

Pure sound language means that it resonates with Light and Truth, so you may understand it to be an 'alive' and 'living' language whose sounds can penetrate through barriers of denser sound as your human thoughts and emotions.

This, as an expression of the Wisdom, allows it to flow through the culture in ways that are extraordinary, as it does in Mother India. Where else upon this planet has one culture, one civilization, held the heart, mind and soul of a whole world? And constantly bathed it and nurtured it through the Wisdom of the Vedas as spoken, sung, and chanted as the Mind and Heart of Pure Sound, as is the Sanskrit language.

And all that is the enigma of India, all of what makes sense — and all of what makes no sense — is truly the enigma of a whole humanity on Earth. There is nothing in Mother India that is not somewhere else as life, as experience and as expression, being lived as part of a system of life, you call culture. Mother India holds it, blesses it and uplifts it.

THE WRITINGS

To be blessed with a lifetime in India is to be blessed with the good karma to uplift — through the language of pure Sound — all life upon your world. Singing God *into* everything, speaking God *as* everything, sending your thoughts into everything to be cleansed. The enigma of India is that it is Heaven on Earth and Earth in Heaven. The home of un-accountable Living Masters for thousands of years, holding Heaven on Earth, holding Earth in Heaven, not forgotten, *never* forgotten.

And all that is the confusion of karma and karmic existence, the Blessed Mother India holds precious to Her Heart.

"If no one else will have you, I will."

She suckles the confused heart at Her Breasts of Love and the Milk of Wisdom flows as a food to nourish the soul of the confused one. And the nourishment builds acceptance as tolerance, as:

"I will make the most of what I have."

And the body may not always have much, but the soul is exhumed in the pure Fires, the healing Water of Life and Language in India, as India. You may not understand the purpose or the need for Mother India on your Earth plane, but it is important all the same.

In the same way the Lands of Egypt were important, and in the same way Greece was important, India is too. And no matter what Great Change looks like as your future, the significance of these civilizations is

Ambition, the Distorter of The Wisdom

never lost and can never be taken from the soul of any living being upon this plane. For no matter where you live in this lifetime, or how many lifetimes you have had, your soul has stitched into it the Wisdom as Life, held within the Light of these original ones, as civilization.

How do you make Truth come to Life in your world? More than ever before, these times you live in are wanting that knowing. It does not matter where you stand politically, economically, and religiously-spiritually, you are wanting the Light to turn on brighter for you. So you can see more clearly what it is you are embracing as your understanding of the Wisdom. It is all too easy to simply hold on to the deciphered pool of wisdom that is being handed to you. You accept without much consideration the deciphering of wisdom by others, not realizing that you are the Wisdom, and your heart is the doorway into your own Temple of Love.

Your conditioned uncertainty has filled you with doubt about this being possible and your lack of understanding of 'how can it be possible'. If you do not see how it can be — and this truly is the key — then it will never be possible.

You cannot build a great civilization in the full meaning of the word 'great' without incorporating the Wisdom within the greatness. And the Wisdom must be alive and living, beyond the ego mind's interpretation and deciphering. The only way this is possible is for there to be an Incarnation of the Wisdom. Incarnate Wisdom says there is a Fountainhead in present time that is the Source of the Wisdom. Incarnate Wisdom has been called God Incarnate because the Wisdom is God. God is the Wisdom.

You, as people of this Earth, want your own understanding of the Wisdom. In the twenty-first century you want it explained to you in a certain way. You want it to be relevant to you as language, as understanding. You want to be able to appreciate it and utilize it in a way that still gives you your life. You may not realise it, but you are looking for your twenty-first century version of the Wisdom as God and God as the Wisdom. You do not want the Egyptian version, the Mayan version, or even Mother India's version. You want your One World Village version as life in the twenty-first century.

You may, if you are a Christian of any denomination, want to remain fixated on Jesus as your Master even though he is no longer incarnate upon this Earth plane. Many religious groups within the present-day Jesus movement have worked to make His Teachings relevant in this century. But, working to make relevant is always an interpretation and a deciphering by those who — may well be sincere and good intentioned, but — are simply immersing themselves in someone else's Wisdom as God, God as Wisdom.

Is Buddha relevant today? Is Jesus relevant today? Is

Ambition, the Distorter of The Wisdom

the original Pharaoh God King relevant today? Are the Greek Gods and Goddesses relevant today? Are the Hindu Gods and Goddesses relevant today?

If you were to simply sit with all these different expressions of The Wisdom, and take from each the cornerstone pieces of Truth, you would find incredible similarities. And where there are differences, you must look to see when and where these differences were created as purposeful deciphering to uphold Ambition.

Ambition is the great distorter of the Wisdom. The Wisdom is about everyone and everything. Ambition is about "me": 'me' individually, 'me' collectively, 'me' as a Nation, 'me' as an empire, and 'me' as a civilization.

Your history books, if you look deep enough, are full of the Great Distorter. All over this world the 'Incarnate Wisdom' has been killed so as to maintain the continuous march of Ambition. Jesus was just one example, and in the West is upheld as the only One as Incarnate Wisdom who suffered death through the hands of Ambition.

Not so.

Today Ambition hides behind the very one it slayed, knowing that in that disguise so much more can be achieved, as Ambition, without ever being truly seen or noticed. So now it simply appears as the march of the faithful even if it is not all the faithful, but the most 'politically' motivated of them. And who is motivating? What is the source of motivation? What is the intent and proposed outcome of such motivation? The distortion of the Wisdom is apparent in all of this Ambition.

The 'Old God' of Judgement has usurped the 'New God' of Love as 'turn the other cheek'. The Testaments of both are now so intertwined that all is forgotten as simple fact: that Jesus came to uplift the old, deciphered wisdom with the new aliveness of, "I am my Wisdom".

This as God Incarnate, this as Living Wisdom, and this as one who knows. Knows that God the Father, God the Mother, are not judgmental.

Jesus spoke, "My Father and I are One". Jesus is not judgmental.

As with the clerics of Old, you may spend all your time disputing each other's deciphering, revealing to everyone that you do not know. And the constantly bargaining mind of the human ego will never know Truth. It will simply want to distort a Living Master's Knowing down to the level of not knowing. Dispute is counted on by Ambition, because it sews such a fog of confusion that Ambition's real work can go on unnoticed.

The Emperors of the Roman Empire are the best example you have of this. Germany also attempted to create Empire by utilizing many of the 'tricks' that

Ambition, the Distorter of The Wisdom

were used by Rome. And now at this time, when Ambition is a global intent looking to a global outcome much must be hidden within Nations, politics and economics. Much must be hidden within racial and religious discrimination. Much must be hidden within sexual discrimination, and much must be hidden by a controlling media entertainment conglomerate.

Ambition has never not been present on your Earth as the aspect of greatness that is only looking towards the self as ego, as the one in the mirror. So, it is about personal aggrandizements as, "How great am I? How great are we?"

Ambition thrives in this mindset. It feeds *on* it and is fed *by* it. It is a vision of life that lacks the knowing of God. It is a vision of life that speaks, "In the absence of God, I will become that through what I believe God to be."

To conceive of God in this way can only ever be done at the level of power. Power that is the wanting to know through becoming the answer to your question. "How great am I? How great are we?"

And each step Ambition takes — to be greater, more encompassing, more compelling, and more controlling — the question always remains: "Is this great enough to be God?"

And in the absence of knowing God as cognized 'I am', there can only be the constant mountain to climb in which power reaches further and further and permeates more and more of life, and all of it for the purpose of feeling Godly. Power in a vacuum, as it is within Ambition, cannot feel God. It can *as perception* feel like God, but it is so infinitesimally small, *as significance*, that it gives no satisfaction at all. In the final analysis it simply becomes the journey of power for power's sake in which God is dead.

Ambition, as life journeyed, as the journey of God — is dead. And God is dead until you begin to open the Heart of Love, the Heart of Life. Your human life will give you opportunities to awaken yourself to the Heart of Love, the Heart of Life. Each one of you who has already experienced one or more of these Openings, knows how life-changing they are. And life change is the Spirit of God in these times. Life change that is the opening of the Heart of Love, the Heart of Life, is the becoming of Incarnate Wisdom.

Each of you who has had 'awakenings' are growing another 'body' as your own incarnation of Living Wisdom. You will know through personal experience that the Heart is pivotal, because without the Heart your greatness — that is the Self as Living Wisdom — is not possible.

Greatness — as it is known — is what is being decided as the consciousness of this world: greatness, that is either the hollowness of ambition as power, or greatness that is the Ganges of India, the living Waters of Truth that nurture the Heart and the Mind to know Wisdom. And then in that, become the incarnation of,

Ambition, the Distorter of The Wisdom

"I am my Wisdom."

Let it be an expansion of awareness in consciousness in which you know love greater, and in that, you love deeper, wider, and longer; in each breath surrounding and permeating each thought, each feeling, each moment of wonder in how beauty, wonder, and magnificence blesses you and all life.

Look to see the greatness you feel in your own heart of love, your heart of life everywhere. See through the distortions being placed before you by your media, communications, and entertainment. See Ambition at work within its own version and vision of greatness. See it for what it is, as exclusive, and then fall inwards to your heart of love and reaffirm greatness as inclusive for everyone everywhere.

Know that the righteous God of Judgement and Power is a distortion perpetuated by its followers. It is not the Truth of the One Beginning, One Truth, and One Wisdom for all as everyone and everything everywhere.

Power, as Ambition, believes at this time on your Earth Plane that it has the winning hand. It believes your world is a gambling house that is within its power to control. And it has gambled — and will continue to gamble — with what it determines to be expendable as life. This is how you will know it and see its existence no matter what 'mask' it is hiding behind. No matter how it is presented to you as 'fact':

as information, as reality, as entertainment, as religious truth, as economic fact, as political fact. All of it is distortion; all of it misleads you and confuses you and causes you to *not* believe in your own greatness as Incarnate Wisdom.

To forget your own 'awakening of the heart', and to brain-drain you with all that is divisive in your world, Ambition is causing you to constantly focus on what is wrong with everything everywhere. It wants you to focus your awareness there, because it knows that what is focused upon then becomes the agreed-upon 'reality'.

This has worked successfully for longer than you would imagine, but at this time the Wisdom is incarnating — and has incarnated — as your teachers, as your writers, as your activists, as your scientists, as certain businesses.

And the meditators as the prayer-filled ones everywhere: praying to the Father, the Mother, the Gods and Goddesses of the Heavens. They are the mystics of Light chanting sacred Sounds into the very foundation of all Life speaking,

"Come forth, Great Change. We welcome it as our own fruitful, blessed awakening. And in service to the One Truth, One Love, One God everywhere for everyone, we open our hearts to greater Life.

Ambition, the Distorter of The Wisdom

And in that, the realization that I, as the One of the One within the One, will uplift the Darkness into the Light.

This I invite, this I call forth. This I pray."

I love you.

So be it.

The Flow of Consciousness

My Beloved One,

Even if you cannot see it happening to you there are things occurring in people's lives everywhere that are dramatic in their power to affect their lives.

Whether it affects the body, mind, or emotions, it imposes on consciousness new and different ways of dealing with life. And this has to be done; there are no other options as you see it, and so you set about acquiring the necessary new habits that will condition you in acceptance that this is how life is now.

And when this happens, as a result of something that has happened to you or someone near and dear to you, there is still the feeling of not knowing what is going to happen next.

But you know a course is set, as a life experience taken on that allows you a certain sense of sureness, as inevitability that something further will unfold from that initial dramatic incident.

This incident in consciousness may occur over a considerable period of time. In consciousness, the change simply *is* and so, in effect, it is timeless. It does not appear or feel that way to you because of your attachments to *Time* as flow, rather than *Consciousness* as Flow.

In your life, Time's effect on your consciousness is seen through 'the play of your lives'. You are not always, in fact rarely, aware when the flow of consciousness was altered. There is always that moment—or those moments—when your considerations about yourself, your considerations about life, as influential, does not indicate that it was isolated and totally unforeseen. No, *highly Influential* means that what had been given a home within you has been gaining power. This power creates influence. Influence turns the page from the expected and anticipated to the *unexpected* and *unanticipated*.

The page is turned as consciousness. What has influence now *becomes* the influence. What was always impacting now ushers in the result. Consciousness flows. The result is the outcome of a particular flow of consciousness.

Consciousness carries thought, carries emotion as flow. Even your most immovable thoughts and emotions have flow. They are flowing somewhere. They are moving into creation to create something, something in your life, something in your body. And the longer the flow continues the more substantial becomes the manifestation, and the greater the longevity you give to your creation.

You live such personal lives in which 'hiding' is a major factor. Hiding from yourself more than anyone

The Flow of Consciousness

else, and that allows you the luxury of 'hiding' from others. Hiding from yourself is the nature of Ignorance, so it is simply who you are as human nature. Human nature, as the consciousness of 'hiding', allows your own hidden thoughts and emotions to have a life, as the flow of consciousness without being aware that it is even occurring.

Depending upon the balance of Influence, this can bring to you the *new*, or allow you to remain in the *old*. In your human lives you can feel stuck or unstuck; either way it is relative, because you are always stuck in a particular flow of consciousness, as repetitiveness, until you realize that you are the power—as Self—that can and will change that. This is you moving through deeper and deeper layers of influence in consciousness as your thoughts and emotions. If you simply move as direction—everywhere and anywhere—then within your own human-nature consciousness you are stuck within repetitiveness. And so flow will move toward whatever that repetitiveness is, as *thought-emotion*, and bring it into manifestation.

What you think and feel, besides being personal, is also public and general. You may call it common because, as beliefs, they are part of your culture, your society. They are part of the times you are living in. So, they may be called the generalized thoughts and emotions held by humanity.

These generalized thoughts and emotions have a flow in consciousness, and it has been referred to as the

THE WRITINGS

River of Consciousness that flows throughout this Plane. And if this River carries the majority of your immovable thoughts and emotions, then flow—as consciousness—will move into the *building* of manifestations and the *sustaining* of those manifestations. How you separate the personal from the general is impossible for you because it is all acquired. Accepted as personal conscious choice, or accepted in personal ignorance in which you are unaware that you even made a choice. You did make a choice. Your ignorance made it for you. That seems unfair and impossible, but all the same it is true. It is the nature of life in this dimension.

What you do about it changes the flow of consciousness. It changes the flow that is personal and the flow that is general. This gives you hope. This permits you to feel there is an alternative: as your flow in consciousness that can change the outcomes …that can change the manifestations.

You want to know how to catch outcomes before they become outcomes. You are wanting to change the intent. You can only change the intent by changing the direction of the flow. You change the direction of the flow by changing the source. To change the source, as intent, you must access a different source as thought and emotion. This source has to live as consciousness beyond your human nature source. For that to be possible you have to consider that there is another nature to be as self, other than your human nature.

The Flow of Consciousness

To consider another source says that you must become someone different, as that source. Someone different, as source, is to entertain and embrace a different consciousness and allow your life to flow in that consciousness as your self-awareness. Self-awareness is a strived-for state that requires brilliance and genius in order to be sustained. These powers are not outside of you, but within you. They are not acquired so much as remembered. Remembering reacquaints you with your own state of Truth in which you accept that this is who you truly are. You are brilliant. You are a genius.

Your difficulties with this, as self-knowing, are present because of your own habitual and familiar flow in consciousness that is your ever-present existence in the flow of time within the confusion and uncertainty of your human nature ignorance. You are always telling yourself—and the world—that this is who you are. You are not remembering anything different. So, change in the flow is not occurring. It is simply not happening.

If it is true that you want this to happen. If it is true that you are unconsciously waiting to have this pointed out as your understanding of where you are at and what needs to happen next. Then here it is, here is an understanding that you may embrace as Truth that gives you a path of Remembering that is solid, real, and true for you. Once this is in place within you, as a new structure, your soul will then begin to work with you more directly. It will be your opportunity to become more of a partnership working with the same goals, with the same intentions to accomplish the same outcomes. Your life takes on new meaning, greater meaning, and in that breathes Life essences into your consciousness that have been called higher purpose.

Higher purpose, as Life essence, always requires the presence of you, as soul. This is your vehicle of association that connects you to your Self as the flow of the Christ Consciousness, the flow of the Buddha Consciousness. This is your re-acquaintance with Power as Love within the flow of Consciousness. This is your re-acquaintance with Certainty within the flow of Consciousness. This is your beginning stage of walking as human, in your life, as the flow of Consciousness that is wholeheartedly and willingly embracing Love, Power, and Certainty as the essence of who you are.

You are awakening. You are remembering. You are no longer asking yourself the question from within your confusion, "Who am I?"

You have 'Knowing' now. You are cognizing as real, as true. "*This* is who I am."

In this, you are realizing the ongoing nature of Manifestation in which Intent and Outcome are the keys that determine what and how and when any particular 'creation' will manifest.

No longer is life seen as something that happens to you, but now you realize your awakening gift, as

The Flow of Consciousness

Grace and Blessing, that is you happening to life. You happening to life, is *you* that effects change. Change outside and beyond the normal flow in the River of Consciousness on this Earth Plane.

In this you become different. You begin to be the 'different' and the 'difference'. Life around you changes. Changes around you cause changes to occur elsewhere. Changes elsewhere cause greater and greater influence, as change, to manifest as new life, new world, new Earth, and new consciousness everywhere.

What do you want to subscribe to as your personal and general intent and outcome? Do you want to work for the One as the incoming Flow of Consciousness? Do you want to set aside differences and work within the Flow of Consciousness that speaks?

"We are the same, we are not different from each other."

Do you want to be active and involved in your own awakening? And in that, do you want to bear witness to the differences, as life, that will manifest all around you? These are the times of greater Light, greater Life, and each of you has come to participate and enjoy the manifestation of a changed you and changed life everywhere on your Earth.

Participation is the key. To participate you must awaken. To awaken you must associate your flow of consciousness with who you are as soul, who you are as the Christ-Buddha Consciousness. This is your decision to awaken to self-responsibility as *intent* and *outcome*. Choice, that is responsibility, is your soul calling to you to awaken. Your resistance to change, that requires you to be present as a self-responsible one for the purpose of your Awakening, is you as human ego self.

You must become aware that your human ego nature wants to interpret your movement into greater Flow in Consciousness as an opportunity to become more powerful. A more powerful ego only allows you the manipulation of yourself and those around you. This will cause drama and conflict to rise in your life because it is your direction as intent. You know you are creating a more powerful ego to brace yourself against those around you, and in that, remain more securely 'hidden'.

Within the Western world you have 'movements' in sections of your culture that feel innately better, innately more awake, more aware, and in that, closer to their true-nature self or their Enlightenment. None of this is necessarily true if it is only information. You may have more enlightened information, but unless you are moving daily into the Flow of Consciousness that transcends information, then you are 'stuck' all the same.

You have to transcend Information in order to become truly self-responsible. Information may grant you more obvious choices, but if you do not enact in self-responsibility, then you are simply creating deeper

The Flow of Consciousness

levels of confusion and conflict that plague your mind and your heart. You will only find new and different ways to be in self-judgement, and all of this can eventually trickle into the mind and the heart of your human nature self, that then allows it to declare, "Who needs this in any case?"

This, as a position of 'stuck-ness', exists within all ego human nature in many different areas of your life and on many different levels. This is the struggle all those on a spiritual path run-up against. This is the 'hidden' wanting to remain hidden. This is lack of self-responsibility wanting to remain not responsible. This is the antagonistic portrayal of life wanting to be left in place as real and true.

This is struggle as the dominant direction of your flow in consciousness. Not just struggle of a human nature kind, within your daily lives, but struggle of a consciousness kind that constantly moves you towards, and then away from, your transcendent experiences. And it is not that you do not want them, but more that you are so easily overpowered by the already existing flow in your consciousness.

Mind, emotion, and physical-altering drugs have been utilized for thousands of years to assist you in slipping through the net — the web of your human ego — and in that find yourself in the Beyond as the flow of consciousness. In these states you may experience yourself, as awareness, differently than you may in your daily life.

THE WRITINGS

Freeing yourself from the grip of the human ego consciousness is the first step, the only step you ever take. But you take that step over and over until you become so familiar with yourself, as that step, that there is nothing that escapes your attention. This is what you are doing as your pathway. You are recovering all that has escaped your attention. This is what Remembering and Awakening is truly all about.

It is this simple.

You are recovering all that has escaped your attention. Your attention, as awareness and as focus, is capable of unlimited expansion. If your attention is held by your beliefs and opinions as the mental and emotional juice they give you, then you are 'stuck' as your attention. You are saying you do not need or want anything else to be attentive to. This is enough.

"This is enough," is the belief—as comprehensive—that you are *only* human. When you are in Heaven you will be only human. When you are in Hell you will be only human. 'Only human' has your total attention. And you cannot even think the thought or feel the feeling to expand beyond it. For many, for most, there is no sense, no awareness of there being anywhere else to go, anyone else to become. And if you are one of those, who through Information, feel you know you have somewhere else to go, someone else to become, you are nonetheless still required to show yourself that you have what it takes to walk the walk rather than simply talk the talk.

The Flow of Consciousness

"How human is still human?"

This question is also the answer, and you are living it. Your life lives within the answer, as the answer. And this will always be so until you exist as Self outside the question. In that you will be living within a new question and your life is the answer.

"How much God is still God?"

This is Transcendence for you. Your Flow of Consciousness is now truly the Flow of Aliveness. Aliveness is Life, all Life: everywhere, above and below, within and without. And Aliveness speaks the Truth.

"I am in it everywhere, as it. I am alive as All Life".

This, as Awareness, is the Divine Self as the Self within All. This is the State of Liberation. Beyond the walls of ego consciousness this is who you are. This is you living Liberated in the Flow of Consciousness that is all Consciousness, all Awareness. This is a whole new adventure in Consciousness, and you will not awaken to it all at once. You will walk the walk of, "How much God is still God?"

This is your Awakening. You will never ever realize the answers to that question from within your human nature consciousness. You, as human ego self, does not comprehend God as a cognized reality. So, "I Know I Am," is not contemplated as self-awareness. It is only when you move into the Flow of Consciousness that is your Liberation that you may know that "yes, even within my human nature self I am still God". It is God not knowing that it is God.

Not knowing is not caring, not wanting to know, not able to know, not important enough to know, and not capable of dealing with this as *Known*. All of this allows you, as human self-identity, to exclude yourself from the Path, as the opportunity that is your personal Awakening.

This allows you to imagine you are making choices when you are simply living in the flow of consciousness that is 'stuck', in which nothing has changed. The choice to change went by relatively unnoticed and uncared about as you simply went with the flow of your own 'stuck-ness'.

This, as a revelation, reveals you to you. You may not care to know; you may be threatened in the presence of the power and preciseness of this revelation as it reveals you to you, and in that confronts you with self-responsibility.

What will you choose? Which way will you swing? What do you want *from* life? What do you want *for* your life? You cannot consciously choose until you address—as contemplation—these questions. You must tread water as your life of mind and emotions. You cannot simply float upon the surface of your life allowing all the different currents to take you in any which direction. Treading water invites you to discover: "How deep am I? How deep do I go?"

The Flow of Consciousness

It is a deeper flow which you will connect with as Consciousness, and the deeper flow will begin to affect what you think about and what you want to feel that is new possibility. And the deeper awareness of what you are sending out to know more about, and what you are receiving back as new input, changes everything that is going on in your surface world, as your life.

The depth is affecting the surface in ways you never imagined, you never thought possible, and you still do not quite understand with your human mind and heart. But you are changing, your life is changing, and you feel more and more emboldened to embrace self-responsibility as your True Nature. You want to, and yet you do not understand why this would be so when you have so strongly resisted it for as long as you can remember.

This is not the self-responsibility that is injected into your survival, fear-generated consciousness, but Self Responsibility that is Service to Life, in which you now know, can only occur as awareness by continually opening yourself into the Flow of Consciousness that is All Life, All Love, All God.

There is no other way. The choice is yours and it lives within you as 'You' constantly. This choice never sleeps, it never rests, and it never goes away. No matter how 'awakened' or how 'asleep' you are this choice is always present on the 'edge of your Consciousness'. For within the choice is the ever-present One you are, serving you, serving Life, serving God.

This is you. You are being served always. This service is ongoing, and it will serve you in ignorance or awakening. It makes no difference for there is no difference. You say there is, as human nature self, but your Presence as Divinity, as the one in the mirror says, "It is all the same as One God, One Love."

Your mind and heart does not accept this, and in that, you are the constant struggle within yourself. This can only be resolved by not attempting to resolve it from within the ego human nature. Instead, you must trust the Flow of Consciousness that is all Life, all Love, all God, and dive into these Waters of Life and know that you will expand, you will awaken, and you will 'Become' again. This is what all Liberation is. It is the Flow of Consciousness eternally present in All you are as Truth.

Bow to that Glory, bow to the Blessings of Knowing this. Bow in Appreciation and Gratitude for the knowing of how much more you truly are as Consciousness, as Self Awareness. God is great. God is good.

I love you.

So be it.

Life Issues

My Beloved One,

Awakening can surprise you at times with where it will take you, and in that, what it will reveal to you. What it will reveal to you about your life and *you* that you had forgotten for the time being. It is not that it was forgotten entirely, but that it went away the last time you dealt with the issue.

Issues are layered within your human nature consciousness. That is why what you think you have already dealt with can return to you. Each time an 'issue' returns there is a great opportunity to expand your awareness of it as you and your life. You may even have awakening glimmers that this issue is larger than this single lifetime.

You know it came to you early in your life, long before you had formed any judgements or opinions about its relative right or wrong. So, the 'issue' simply fell into place in your life, and you simply went with what was presented to you. In such instances you may not have checked in to see whether there was a deeper response to the circumstances that you are not familiar with. And if you sense nothing or felt nothing other than, "I am having this experience," it may not have been recognized as one of your life issues.

Life issues, as different levels of consciousness, can be soul issues or human mind and heart issues. Human mind and heart issues can be formulated by the family, the church, and the society. They can hold the blueprint that is used to judge circumstances as they come into your life. This can be a source of conflict for you that at some point in your awakening you will have to be released from. The soul issues are much more intimate. In that, they have a familiarity that is smooth and slippery causing you to easily slide, as life direction, into the heart of the issue.

Before you could even contemplate it, before you were old enough to contemplate it, before you realized there was a need to contemplate anything, you simply went 'there' and became the experience as your life.

Some issues do not seem to have boundaries. These are soul issues. Soul issues that can be labelled by your culture and society as good or bad, right or wrong, safe or dangerous. What is true is that soul issues are journeys you are familiar with, a little familiar or highly familiar. And in that familiarity, you are discovering all of who you can be as possibility within that soul issue. The issue did not begin as an issue. Within the soul it began simply as journey. There was innocence, and there was ignorance. There was life to be known.

Life to be known in your Divine State of Existence is

truly the question, "Is God this too? Is this good enough to be God? Will I know myself as God within this experience?"

God always speaks:

> *"I will. I must, for there is only the One.*
> *It is all the One God."*

The 'issue' factor within any experience is when the 'God factor' becomes forgotten. Your human nature ego consciousness is an 'issue-based' consciousness, as that it is key to creating and resolving any issue. The human ego must resolve by absolving. And dissolving must, as forgiveness, be given to the ego nature to assist it in its task of dissolving 'issues'.

The ego nature must elevate as identity the 'I am' into the state of your True Nature. Within that nature you may declare,

> *"I am forgiveness. I am acceptance, and I am Love."*

When you find, as your awakening, the 'issue' consciousness of your human ego nature moving front and center, you know there is forgiveness to exercise. You know there is acceptance to honor. And you know there is Love to *be*. Any 'issue' that is constantly recycling through your consciousness as you awaken, signifies another level of forgiveness, acceptance, and Love that must be given and received to all that is the 'issue' and all and everyone who has ever participated with you in this or any other 'issue'.

THE WRITINGS

This Power as forgiveness, as acceptance, as Love allows you to penetrate the Veil of Ignorance that holds as belief that this is only about 'me' now in this lifetime. And, as expanded consciousness, cups the soul in the hands of forgiveness, acceptance, and Love. Soothing the journeys held, as 'issues' still stuck within. Everything that is your life is an 'issue' that you are wanting to elevate within.

The whole purpose of your human existence is to elevate your consciousness. To elevate the consciousness is your 'issue-by-issue' awakening. And your human heart and mind cannot know all of your issues. Only your soul knows them and holds them for you in the Love of the Christ-Buddha Consciousness you are. Your human heart and mind lives within each issue as those issues.

Your subconscious mind is the mind of your issues. The mind and heart in each lifetime take on a new iteration, a new costume, in which to dress up and talk about and judge the 'issue'. Because your mind and heart are from — and of — this lifetime only. It believes this is the one and only time you have ever confronted this 'issue'.

Not so, your soul is holding it as Journey in Ignorance. Therefore, the human mind and heart can be confounded by the truth of your 'issue'. This is what your teachers, healers, and therapists are wanting you to grasp. You must elevate your consciousness beyond blame and justification. Even if you do not believe in reincarnation, but accept the existence of the soul, consider then that 'issues', in any lifetime for anyone are challenges given to you by your soul for the purpose of dissolving judgement through the power of forgiveness, allowance, and Love. And in that, return this experience of life back to the oneness of all, as Life.

No one has an 'issue-free' existence, everyone is challenged. You may not like your issues and may prefer someone else's. You may look at their issues and believe that you could do better with those issues than with your own. But you only have your 'issues'.

They are what you have as your life to experience. What you achieve, as power within these issues, is completely up to you. No one can do it for you. This is the essence of self-responsibility that is your path of awakening. It is to dissolve the issues in the presence of forgiveness, allowance and Love.

This sounds so simple, but you know that it is not through your own personal experiences. You know you struggle even to identify your issues. You are much more comfortable identifying the issues in your family members, friends, acquaintances, and complete strangers. You are more 'switched on', more aware of other people's issues than you are of your own. Judgement blinds you to the issues within you, and yet, the same judgement highlights these issues within others.

THE WRITINGS

Judgement then must be viewed as the walls of your own defensiveness. Defensiveness blinds you to the possibility of looking and seeing anything within yourself. Your human ego uses defensiveness to draw down the shades to hide your issues from the light of possible awareness. This allows you to flatline as consciousness and in that state you never really deal with your life as 'issues' handed to you in each lifetime by your soul.

You do, however, constantly bicker, rant, and rave about issues of conditioning that have flavored your personality in ways that others like or dislike, find attractive or unattractive, desire to be critical of or defensive of. This is the superficial bargain you make with each other. Unconsciously, you want it to be this way for the safety it provides you, and the 'hiding' that is allowed to continue within you, as you.

How do you overcome this life pattern that, to you, is the nature of being human? Life patterns will never be addressed until you are *ready* to address them. Readiness is not the one that is you waking up one morning and declaring to the world, "I am ready to address my issues."

Unfortunately for your human ego self it is more likely that readiness is the constant placement of yourself within your issues that forces you, as a propelling power, to move away and out of.

'Away and out of' is not the running away that you

Life Issues

have already engineered as the answer to your problems. This ego 'trick' has not advanced you in your awareness of how to move beyond the issues. So, readiness at some point becomes the giving up of the fight to stay one step ahead of any issue. One step ahead of any issue as an ego game sets you up in a cat-and-mouse game with your soul. And it is a game you can never win; you lack the conscious awareness. Your only way is to fake winning by becoming numb, as defensiveness, to the power of any issue.

You know it is there, but you choose to ignore it. You choose to play ignorant; you choose to ignore the call to change. And in that, you immerse yourself, time after time, in the consciousness of judgement in which 'issues' are simply acknowledged as a fact of life. And in that, you realize that you are addicted and enjoy talking about another's issues—and your own—as if it is all there is to do.

"This is the way human ego nature is." Yes, and what do you want to accept as who you are by nature?

This is a profound question. Worthy of your continual consideration. For it will tell you exactly how submerged you are within your 'issues' as your daily life. It will reveal to you how willing or unwilling you are to deal with your life as your 'issues'. It will reveal to you your perceived problems and challenges in dealing with them. You will, at some point, run into your own personal world of fear. What you fear to lose, and what you fear to gain. What you are not ready to accept about yourself that is painful and what you are not ready to accept about yourself that is brilliant as Life.

Your pain is held within each and every issue. Your brilliance is held within the 'authorship' of each issue. Authorship is the Mind and the Heart of God that speaks,

> *"This all began within Love looking for greater Love. This all began within Consciousness as the One looking to know a more profound Consciousness as greater awareness, greater appreciation, and greater Love."*

Your 'issues' live as 'aliveness' within the Dual Nature of Mother-Father God as the Beginning One. You do not understand how your issues can be so important, so profound, and so significant in the Whole of God. They are that because there is only God.

I say it again. There is only God. And once again. There is only God. There is nothing outside of the One Beginning and Mother-Father God. All is within God, as God.

This is you. This is who you are. This is what your life truly is, in its most expansive experience and expression. Within God, as God, you are all of this as Life, as Existence.

Your 'issue' consciousness, as a stuck consciousness, is one of judgement. Judgement of journeys taken *within* your soul, *by* your soul. They are, in the totally expanded consciousness of the One, truly just a drop

Life Issues

of water, a grain of sand in the *Allness* of you as the One Self by many Names, with many Faces, within the many forms of Lord God and Goddess.

Your 'issues' as detail, in this understanding, live in the shadows of your own Ignorance, that find it too challenging, too much of a change to embrace the Conscious Self as forgiveness, as allowance, and as Love. And use these gifts as your True Nature to propel you into greater and greater conscious awareness of who you are as the One Self in God, as God.

You must be willing to hear this. That is your first step. To know you are so great, so magnificent. You may use this Truth, as Wisdom, to feed your heart and mind as human, with greater possibilities, as awakening, from within your personal sense of being lost. The human ego nature as Ignorance is the consciousness of being lost.

Can you be God and still be lost?

Yes! You must know this, and find comfort in this realization. For in this you know that being lost and being God is not incompatible, it is possible. Why is it possible? How is it possible? It is possible because you have made it so. You have declared it to be possible. And you are living in the embrace of that possibility.

Does your life seem too ordinary, too human to have anything to do with you being God? Yes and no. Yes because your perceived awareness of God is distant and removed from you in your life, as confusion. And no, because your journey in confusion is an Illusionary Dream that your physicality makes 'real' for you.

That, within every essence of your third-dimensional nature, you are existing within a tiered and layered expression of Light and Sound that is in its pure beginning state, still the One God, One Existence, One Beginning. Father Mother God. This Beginning Oneness created itself as Expression. Expression took form. God as Formless, God as Form, whilst still remaining in — and as — the All God.

All expansion is as perception is as awareness, God the Beginning One expanding within the One Great Self as Source. But the expansion, as experience, can only occur within God as Form. So, any realization of expansion is you expanding into more of what God always is, and already is, as the Formless.

There are no limits really to God as Form. And you, in human life, have reached into God as Form and created yourself and your life as God in Ignorance of itself as Formless. You are so immersed in God as Form that you know only Form as real, whilst God as Formless is the question mark. You, as the Formless, is a question mark.

This is the level to which you have delved into how much Form as Consciousness is still God?

"If I *do this* as Form, is it still God?"

"If I *become this* as Form, is it still God?"

Life Issues

As human, your Ignorance is so profound that you are unaware of the Question Mark that you are as God in Form.

As the Christ-Buddha Consciousness you are living in the conscious Awareness of God, as Form, and God as the Formless. This is the Christ-Buddha State of Existence within Consciousness. Your Awakening is your retrieval of the lost awareness of God as Formless, as Self within, and as the One God of All and Everything.

What you are living in, as your life, is what you are saturating as God in Form. You must saturate yourself. You are compelled to drink from the experience until the 'awakening' occurs that speaks,

"This is enough now. I know I must move on."

Your movement is a Calling from within your soul that is being used as a megaphone by the Christ-Buddha Consciousness to direct you to your next level of experience. Is it a new experience altogether? Is it another level of experience of something you have experienced before?

It can be any and all of these, depending upon the push to know more Life that is held within the Lord God-Goddess Consciousness, as your Beginning Purity and your Beginning Quest to know the Beginning Oneness within both the Formless and the Form.

Such lofty contemplations, such Wisdom, will unsettle the human nature Ignorance; and from within it the unsettling can be experienced as a positive or a negative ... or a mixture of both. The Journey is so grand, and you feel so insignificant, you may wonder whether it really matters or whether your efforts will truly be noticed.

Such a level of doubt is only possible within a nature that is constantly bathing itself in its own ignorance and confusion. A nature that has settled for a compromise it is unaware it even made. Your belief that you are only human is a consciousness you have settled into as a state of awareness in which you know nothing different, nothing more, and nothing else.

This is neither good nor bad, right or wrong. It simply is. It is simply you, experiencing life and your world at the level it presents itself, as a realm of Existence within God as Form. You are 'asleep' to God as Formless, and you are asleep to God as Form. That is okay, because it only lasts for as long as it does. Eventually, at some point in time your soul will indicate to you the arrival in Consciousness of your need to:

"Wake up, Buddha."

The sound of Life within your life will change. The Light of Life within your life will change. You are being penetrated. You are being Called, Your Journey as the One God within the Formless and the Form is being pulled — as Consciousness — into a state of Awakening in which your soul is now directing your

Life Issues

life into experiences that assist you to:

> *"Wake up, Buddha."*

Once this Divine Transition in Consciousness is initiated within the Lord God-Goddess State, your journey in Time takes on new meaning. The new meaning is your personal experience of awakening within your human life. You may find this incredible, astounding, and amazing that you and your life — that you believe in ignorance to be so insignificant — is now being penetrated by the Author of this Incredible Journey of,

> *"I Am, You are, We are."*

The immense Conscious Awareness of you, as Author, as 'I Am' is reaching into the story of Journey that is compiled and held within you as soul, reaching into this lifetime, now, and calling you to congratulate you on brilliance performed, brilliance experienced, and brilliance in Ignorance. Now the Great One is calling, as Invitation, as a compelling passion.

> *"Bring this all Home to Me,*
> *My Beloved One, you are 'I Am'."*

You are living now in this mix of consciousness. You are trying with your human mind and heart to interpret what is going on in your consciousness. You are struggling to make sense of how to translate this into life direction and life choices.

You are wondering how meaningful within you is this

growing passion, this growing curiosity, this growing compulsion to make changes.

This, no matter the detail—as Wisdom—is the Awakening that is being called for from within the Christ-Buddha Consciousness as the Master of Formless and Form. This is the focus of collection. You and your soul as the Christ-Buddha Partnership are collecting every last experience you have ever journeyed, and as they are collected—as journey, as contemplation—you bring to them the Intent of the Formless God you are.

"I give to All this the Love I Am."

And in that Love, you, as the Christ-Buddha Awareness, hold all and every journey you have ever journeyed in the everlasting presence of forgiveness, of allowance, of gratitude and appreciation, of peace and of Love.

This is you as Self Realized knowing that it is all God, God the Formless, and God as Form. You are the brilliant expression and experience, the brilliant knowing of both. And in that, you reside within the One *as* the One.

God is Great, God is Good.

I love you.

So be it.

Understanding Duality in God as God

My Beloved One,

The Dual State of Consciousness allows you to live aware, in the visible world of Earth, and the invisible worlds of expanded Consciousness simultaneously. This is how you know that God is Dual in Nature, and as that Nature is everything and all things. The Dual Nature of Time and No Time knows that everything is *from* the Beginning, *within* the Beginning. Its essence, its root, is still in the Beginning as the ever-present Beginning in which nothing is created, nothing is destroyed. In this state of the One there is All God.

What you choose to make of this Wisdom, as Truth, is always up for intellectual debate, and this can only occur in the barren and infertile mind of 'only human'. The mind of the human cannot understand Duality in God as God. Authority must be orchestrated by those who are invested in maintaining a 'reality' in which God is not dual in Nature. This orchestration has always been focused on a desire to maintain the state of ignorance of the Divine Self, ignorance of your own Dual Nature. Such a focus allows you to be 'told' what is true and not true. What you must accept as Faith and what you must believe because it is written in this

THE WRITINGS

Book or that Book, all of which carries the imprimatur of 'sacred', of 'truth', of originating in the Divine.

All such writings when written by 'disciples of' — rather than the Source who cognizes Truth and is that Truth — are filled with interpretation. And for thousands of years these 'sacred' Books have been, and are still being, reinterpreted by those who are a conscious state within 'the mind of ignorance'.

Humanity's innocence, hope, and willingness to believe has been corralled by those who would feed them fairy-tales masquerading as 'teachings', masquerading as a 'truth-filled documentation' of events, circumstances, and relationships. And above all, these 'teachings' are completely bereft, empty, lacking the power to unseat the consciousness from its non-dual state and move it into the liberated state of the Dual Nature of Self.

Is this by accident or design?

You may answer this for yourself. The outcome, either way, is that you have been placed as human self in a very stuck world of thought and emotion, in which there is very little movement in consciousness. Part of 'waking up' is to begin to be aware that the 'only future' being handed to you by those invested in orchestrating your existence is to have you continuously living in a state of overwhelm in which you simply bow down and accept your lot in life, and what is being handed to you, as your existence. To live

Understanding Duality in God as God

your life within this framework controls all your dreams of influence, all your dreams of contribution and all your dreams of,

"What I want my life to be."

Whatever are your upper limits of dreaming, without the introduction as Wisdom, of the Dual Nature of Self, then you will only quest for self-realization in a human interpretation, in which you set goals and go after them as if there is nothing else, and that nothing else matters. This, as non-dual God, leaves you as a nature that is all about life and death, beginnings and endings. It leaves you at the mercy of *Time,* and all that affects you as experiences *in* Time and *through* Time. You are perishable. You are given a perishable nature to live within, and when you die you are given a heaven and hell as after-life in which you will never be more than human, as a human being, human soul, human heaven, and human hell. This is the non-dual nature of Existence that you are being handed, and then stroked and soothed and told,

*"This is enough. Be happy. Find hope,
find peace, and find everlasting life in this."*

What you have been and are being handed as your 'fate', as the 'meaning of your life' to accept and to live within is now being entered by Truth as the Dual Nature of the Self. You are being entered by You. The human self is being influenced and affected by the Divine Self. The microcosm by the macrocosm, and the macrocosm is being influenced by the microcosm. Smaller than the smallest, larger than the largest, Life in all its True Nature is coming for you.

The Vedas of Ancient Times, the Seers who cognized purely the Truth of Life, the Truth of the One Beginning that is Dual in Essence, Dual in Nature, are coming alive within your consciousness. As that occurs all 'interpretations' of Truth will fall by the wayside. And you will leave them lay where they are, so intently are you focused on the brilliance you are as Self. And your awareness of this is growing and expanding as Felt Awareness *in* your consciousness, *as* your consciousness. You are no longer alarmed. You are excited, happy, and fulfilled. Your peace and joy are as contagious as yourself and your life. And you know that this is purpose for you, realizing God as Self, as happiness and joy, compassion and peace. You are that. You feel it as giving and receiving. It is the Tao of your life, the Tao of your Self. The Tao of the One Life that is the Vedas.

"Life I am. Life I am. Life I am."

'Life I am' speaks, "God is Dual. The Beginning One is Dual. This is the Father; this is the Mother."

This you are expanding into. You, as a humanity of souls, are expanding into it as consciousness. Every living being is expanding into it. God as Dual is the very Breath of the Golden Age of Enlightenment you have now entered.

Understanding Duality in God as God

Rejoice,

"Veda. Veda. Veda. Life I am. Life I am. Life I am."

You want to allow in more Life, but you never knew how to, or even if it was possible. But your embrace of the Wisdom of Duality gives you somewhere to reach and expand into that is not simply the ladder of success handed to you by your economic machine.

This is what will open you to life possibilities that include God, include Spirit, and include the soul because in Duality as Divinity, all that surrounds you as Life, everything without any exclusion is in God as God.

Ignorance makes sense now. You understand it as the Perceptual Worlds of God's Nature as that Nature. Understanding, forgiveness, and compassion makes more sense now. Gratitude and appreciation makes more sense now. Human 'love' and unconditional Love makes more sense now. You are everything. What you are currently experiencing as life is not the be-all and end-all for you. Duality as God, as Life, gives you a fit that allows you to both accept your present level of awareness, and at the same time make movement into 'greater'.

When you are ready to hear this you will know that greater is liberating and freeing, and opens you to worlds of possibilities for yourself that you had never dared to consider. Such possibilities are your Divine Inheritance, your Divine Birthright. It is your

THE WRITINGS

Beginning within The One.

All of this — as words — can overwhelm the mind that is only human, because it has accepted all the conditioning, all the indoctrination for a lifetime ... indeed lifetimes. This is the 'you' that is downtrodden even when you do not know it, even when you do not accept it, even when life within the economic machine calls you 'successful'.

You have been clever enough and smart enough to 'survive' in the system. But you had to 'die to your Self' in order to achieve that. And you may be conscious of your 'closing of the Eyes of Knowing' or you may be so ruled as consciousness by "I have done the right thing", that the defensiveness rears up to protect that one, as you from the hidden pain of having to make that choice as life, as direction. Knowing that you had to forgo the nourishment of Spirit that is only truly possible whilst you openly commune within that Nature as Self, as who you *are* and who you *want*, as more of your Self.

More of your Self is only possible once you break free of the boundaries for your heart and mind that is your containment within, "I am only human."

This containment is your containment within Survival. Survival, emotionally and mentally, is all about fear. Fear drives everything. All of your other emotions will be derived from the base fear as uncertainty. Fear and uncertainty drive all your actions and reactions. It

Understanding Duality in God as God

drives your intent and, therefore, your outcomes. It colors your life exactly the way you find yourself within it. You are a prisoner to your fear and uncertainty as non-dual God, non-dual self.

You are stuck.

And the questions you have—the enquiry you sense as a power within you—must be questioned, must be made to go to 'sleep', so that you may use that argumentative nature, as fear and uncertainty, to bury the possibilities beyond conscious awareness. Until you begin to awaken, this is the limited appreciation you exist within as movement in consciousness. And, in truth, you must admit that it is little or no movement at all.

In this state, your future—everyone's future, the Earth's future—is foreseeable as your linear projection from where you have stood and still now stand. This is your human perceptual world in which you are seated upon the rocking horse of life's movement in which everything is constantly being played out as hopelessness, hopeful, hopelessness, hopeful: backwards and forwards.

You believe you can exercise your human mind to discipline the effects of this within your emotional state. But the sacrifices you make in pursuing such a course is the loss of the felt awareness as happiness and joy, compassion and peace.

To live outside this Felt Nature of the Self means that

you will continue to create for yourself a life that is out of balance, that is not in harmony with the Movement of Life. A Movement that lives naturally within gratitude and appreciation, forgiveness of self and all others, and the heartfelt upholding of the awareness that all Life is precious. All Life is of The One.

Disharmony will affect your mind. Disharmony will affect your emotional state. And this then affects the health of your physical body. Your body is created as a reflection of peace and harmony, of Love and self-approval, of happiness and joy. Longevity in the body, for your body, is a natural state of harmony. Survival consciousness is not harmonious for the body. It is not a consciousness in which the body can be nourished and thrive as an ongoing healthy, happy life.

True agelessness is a state of Consciousness. It is not a cosmetic product or surgery that simply changes the look of what you see in the mirror whilst the cells of the body remain in the state of 'hopeful, hopelessness', unsure of who you are. And in that, the constant unsureness of,

> *"Can I be loved; will I be loved?"*

This is the bottom-line obviousness of your confusion and doubt. This is a path you have chosen when there has been no other option offered to you. Now, at this time, the choice will be made remarkably and astoundingly clear for you and all life on your world.

You are Dual in Nature. You are human, and yet you

Understanding Duality in God as God

still remain Divine. Your purpose is to reconnect with the Divine Nature you are. You have embraced only one of your Natures, and in that, you have disharmony. This is the time when you are being reacquainted with your other Nature, your True Nature. This is you, as awareness—beyond the perceptual worlds of doubt, confusion, and fear—in which your mental and emotional state has succumbed to the imbalance in your life as Survival Consciousness.

What you want to do about this is not completely clear to you, but as the Age of Awakening continues to manifest a higher vibratory frequency for life upon your world and Mother Earth, you will feel a compulsive need to do something: at some time, somewhere, somehow. You will have to jump outside the box of your current human nature and human existence.

This becomes your 'Leap of Faith' guided by your heart, guided by your soul. Unaccustomed as you are to trust in either your heart or your soul, there are no other options that have not already revealed to you the obviousness of your state of pain and suffering. You can no longer live immersed in such energies. You must fly from that state—and uplift your life from that world—and into a new, but not yet clearly defined alternative.

This is your opportunity to define more clearly the Felt world you choose to create a life within. This will, in partnership with your soul, reveal to you your dharma—as your life path—that you have come to fulfil. It has been hidden from you by your lesser perceptions of life that have created a denser experience of life for you and everyone in your world. Now this Great Change is upon you as a shift in world consciousness. This is unavoidable and inevitable. What you do in response to this shift is your responsibility. It is up to you.

The air you breathe will carry a different vibration. This different vibration, as higher energy, carries the blood-filled higher-vibratory oxygen to every part of your body. The effect, even on the brain and the heart, will be so noticeable that you will be astounded at how you feel, and the positivity of the mindset you are experiencing. Choose Life in these times, in these moments, in these experiences, for this is the Truth of the magnificence, beauty, and harmony that Life truly is when freed from the consciousness of fear and uncertainty.

Freeing yourself has existed in your unconscious state as desire, as fulfilment always. It is the presence of Life that you cannot truly ever escape from, even though you may go to 'sleep' and not be aware of this presence. Now you are awakening to this presence, you are awakening to this freedom that exists for you once you free yourself from fear and uncertainty and all the emotional and mental paraphernalia that goes with it.

Understanding Duality in God as God

This is the Walk of Life that you are upon right now. Each step you take is an opportunity to awaken to higher possibilities for you and your life. Greater possibilities means that there is a greater contribution that you can make to Life, and in that contribution there is a greater receiving you can have that will give you a more powerful conviction of the greatness of the path you are upon.

This, as the Circle of Life, will inspire and encourage you to attain greater heights of self-realization as you ask the question,

> *"Who else am I, as conscious awareness?*
> *Who else am I, as self-awareness?"*

And your 'old world' you lived within as 'only human' will get smaller and smaller in significance and importance as you concentrate your focus *within* and *upon* the Higher Kingdoms that are opening to you. Each of you, as your soul self, will have your own journey, your own unique experiences even though the consciousness that this is contained within is the same for each and every soul.

It is Love. It is peace. It is harmony and compassion. It is Love that is the letting go of all the details that are called history or story, and in its place will simply be the presence of compassion and forgiveness for yourself and all others.

This you overlay over each story, all your history and each and every character that played any role at all

THE WRITINGS

within your 'play of consciousness'.

As you awaken you will more readily and easily take ownership of your history and your stories. You will see the conglomerations of your own perceptions about yourself, life, and others that created it in the first place. You may call it your karmas. You may call it your conditioning. No matter what you call it, you are moving beyond it. The tentacles of attachment are being released as you are being unplugged from, "I am only human."

And in that, your Dual Nature can lightly touch down in your consciousness. You are ready now to have both. To know both and accept that,

"I am both. I am human and Divine. I am Dual in Nature. In this, I am free to explore and expand into forever."

I love you.

So be it.

Everyone's Life Path will turn a corner

My Beloved One,

Arriving at this stage in your life is auspicious for you and this world.

You have come into this lifetime to reaffirm a commitment you have made over and over through lifetime after lifetime. You spoke in each one of them, in a humility of prayer-filled love, that you would create a life of testament, in which all of your endeavors — as personal expression and experience — would elevate the consciousness of life within you, life around you, and life everywhere.

You are not new to this focus in this lifetime and within your heart of love you know this to be true. You have spent lifetimes in Service to God, bringing others with you for as far, and for as long, as they could come. And in each lifetime your love of life, your love of humanity has grown stronger, clearer, purer, and more potent. Your stage for this lifetime is as great as you can imagine and as great as your existence here on your Earth will allow.

For your love knows no boundaries of politics or religion, color or race, age or gender. You have come as God has willed it. You are, for Father One Mother One, the manifestation of their Love as All Love. Your own awakening into Love, as Love, is triggering within your soul a greater awareness of 'you' beyond the state of physical autonomy.

What lives within your soul as *you*, is now 'appearing' in your life and, more importantly, within you. So, the borders of Separation are beginning to melt away, and in that, there is a journey and a merging. And in that, you are awakening a Self who exists within another 'body' and, in time, other bodies.

For now, your stage of awakening is within one other body, one other life: one that you call, as your understanding, your Beginning Soul Mate. Your life force has been aroused by this 'discovery', this awakening, even if you are not yet completely able to register consciously all of the different aspects of your being that are resonating to this expanded life force. You do not have to try to understand it, for in perfect timing it will all just happen. You are now upon your path of expanding into Love, focused intently upon your Beginning Love, that you call your Father, your Divine Precious Mother.

Around and around, you are weaving an ever-expanding conscious relationship with Mother Father, Father Mother, One. You know this can never end, for indeed it feels to your conscious mind like it has only just begun. But it has not. Through so many lifetimes you have weaved your unique and outrageous Love

Everyone's Life Path will turn a corner

within The Two that is The One Beginning. So much so that you cannot separate The Two. You cannot acknowledge one without acknowledging the other. So around and around you speak "Father Mother, Mother Father."

You have already contemplated how this has blossomed into your conscious awakening at this point along your path, and are continuing to do so. You see within your life how certain experiences, as dots, have been connecting themselves together with stringlets of Light. And within each experience you have created greater and greater opportunities for 'ah ha' moments in which to expand your awareness into another stage, and a new development in your conscious awakening.

You are now consciously marveling at what is going on in your path, as your path. You are beginning to clearly sense its uniqueness, and the uniqueness of your own awakening. No matter how you describe this experience as feelings and awareness, you will find it making less and less sense to try and have another — or others — appreciate this journey. More and more it can, and will, feel like greatness and madness all rolled into one. So, words become incapable of bridging the chasm called knowing and not knowing.

Words cannot inject knowing, only experience can give knowing. For someone who has gathered knowing through experience, then words can be the acknowledgement of the 'ah ha' in which you speak spontaneously with utter conviction,

"I know this to be true for me too."

The words were simply the vehicle that carried to you the 'ah ha' moment in which you knew, "I am not alone". The purpose of all higher Wisdom is to be there for you when you arrive at a certain stage of your awakening so that you may know clearly, brilliantly, lovingly, and peacefully that, "I am not alone".

The journeys of each soul, as individual awakening, are to gain a stronger, and more vital, and alive hold on the Truth as Union. The "I am not alone" you have also carried within you for the lifetimes of journey, in which you have only felt and declared, "I *am* alone."

This is life as the consciousness within dimensions of 'reality' we call Separation.

To not know Merging, to not know Union is to be alone. To be alone is not something that is always openly acknowledged, except in the hearts and minds of the desperate ones. It is, however, always present within all your life expressions and experiences. All of your stories and all of your history, "I am alone" is seated there in the very heart of your human soul.

The brilliant quests you journey in each lifetime are really the covering over and camouflaging of, "I am lonely".

So, if I do this, do that, be this, be that, become this,

Everyone's Life Path will turn a corner

become that, I will bury and hide the pain of "I am alone."

Love is the only Path that is limitless, and as that, can liberate you as consciousness from "I am alone."

Your path is your awakening to Love, and in that, the baby fledgling awakenings that are removing you from the consciousness of "I am alone."

For the longest time, even as a spiritualist, you are living within "I am alone" whilst committing yourself to practices on a daily basis, that you—without knowing exactly how or when—are praying to be liberated as the knowing. And within your spiritual practices there exists, if directed, the inner way of Selfless Service in which all Life, all souls everywhere, are included. The more you include all Life—all souls everywhere—you are telling your soul,

> *"I am reaching for God. I am reaching for my Beginning.*
> *I am reaching for The Beginning to have and to hold*
> *and be one within my Father my Mother,*
> *my Mother my Father, as The One."*

This is the awakening into the great Self you are. In this journey, "I am alone" fades away and dissolves as thought emotion. You have elevated, refined, and gone beyond it as the basis for your life and your path. It is no longer who you are as 'Becoming'.

You reside inside a Consciousness in which Love and Light emanate from within you and all around you. Although you may still be 'seen' as a human body, you are living within that body as another more grand and glorious expression and experience ... as Light and Love. Everyone's life path will, in this lifetime or another, 'turn a corner' and head off in a completely different direction. This may happen more than once for some souls. And it can happen for your human life *and* your spiritual life. And one can take your path into the other. All of this 'turning a corner' is important and significant to your destiny in this lifetime.

Mother-Goddess Pre-Eminence is waiting for you at the 'corner', guiding you towards the 'corner' and is there already as every facet of the 'corner'.

This means her Pre-Eminence is within your consciousness as that 'corner'. Mother Father One, are there to illuminate the 'corner' so that you may clearly see the path you are on that has brought you to it. And the active ingredients in your consciousness are creating a 'corner' where you must decide to turn — or to continue on as before.

'Turning the corner' is your adoration of Life. It is profound. So, in this perceptual world of 'illusions' the Mother Goddess Adoration can be created as manifestations to catch your attention and captivate your awareness, connecting you to Her in such a way that you become 'involved' in Her *Shakti* as Creation. Every time you have ever had an experience of life in which you knew you had to go 'this way', or go 'that way', or go 'after this', or go 'after that' as 'exhilarating life' you were totally involved in the Adoration of Life, as Mother Goddess. The illusion was — and is always — the 'packaging' as the make-up, the dress, the shoes, the hair, the 'walk', the body language, to draw you in as a spider to its web.

Adoration as Life Essence has both a Father flavor and a Mother flavor. It has a Lord God flavor and a Goddess flavor. And in this world of humanity, it has a Man flavor and a Woman flavor. Adoration as Mother Goddess Pre-Eminence is far more mysterious than Father Lord God Adoration. Father, Lord God, is simple, easy, open and clear through the Great Spirit of the One. So, it is direct and purposeful in its obviousness. Adoration as Mother Goddess is pulling you into the very depths of all that is Her Life, as Creation.

So, it is complex and changeable, filled with imagery that can give you a taste, but not the whole experience. If you want the whole experience, you must be prepared to take Adoration at whatever level it is revealed to you through Her Mysteries, and then feel the path within it as to where you are drawn to go to next.

Within Mother Goddess Adoration you are constantly dealing with 'imagery' as manifestations of Her Shakti, as Love, as Power. Within the imagery is the constancy of the invitation to seek Her out through Surrender, as Power. The Mother is the Sacred *Yoni* drawing you in deeper and deeper, and within that experience the heightened revelations of Her Truth,

Her Nature, Her Essence, and Her Power. You are journeying into deeper and deeper layers of Adoration, and this gives to you Her Ecstasy and the ongoing-ness of Life as Orgasmic, in which She reaches for you to pull you in. You become Her. She becomes you. Living in the Experience. Being the Existence of Pure Life Force experienced as the Mother Essence, as Surrender within Power, as Pure Love.

To have this knowing of Her Mystery you must become Her Nature. You must become the Consciousness of Surrender within Power. This is your experience of "I am Love" from within Mother Goddess.

The Father Illumination as Pre-Eminence is different to Mother Illumination as Pre-Eminence. Even though within The One — as Yin and as Yang — the Mother Essence is present within Father Pre-Eminence, as is Father Essence within Mother Pre-Eminence. Present yes, but not of equal focus. This is what the Beingness of Pre-Eminence within the *Tao* is, as momentum and movement, within the Circle of Life. Cycles within cycles to manifest through time and space as the grand opportunity for continually balancing and harmonizing Life as the All Present One. In time and space harmonizing and balancing as movement and momentum requires journey, requires action, requires Spirit in process, emotion in process, and thought in process.

This procession, as movement and momentum in

Everyone's Life Path will turn a corner

consciousness is the life experience of every living being through each soul journeying the ebb and flow of Father Pre-Eminence and Mother Pre-Eminence. Within your own life, you may feel that your spiritual awakening, as a journey, is easier within Father Pre-Eminence. Some may feel, without truly knowing for sure, that the journey of spiritual awakening would be easier within the essences of Mother Pre-Eminence.

As your soul's awakening, you will hold 'knowings' within its upper casing as the soul's Divine Essence, which previous lifetimes have given you as an opportunity for spiritual awakening. And whether those opportunities were opened to as personal journey within either Mother Pre-Eminence, or Father Pre-Eminence, or a mixture of both.

The prolific nature of Life, as all Existence, grants to each soul unimaginable—to the human-conditioned mind and emotions—opportunities to experience Life, as either Mother or Father Pre-Eminence, to enrich the nature of Life experiences that each soul is looking to participate in.

The journeys, as soul, within either Pre-Eminence is determined through The Lord God Goddess of your Being, and their Gateway. The combined Influences of each Pre-Eminence brings back to Lord God Goddess the bounty of each lifetime's journey. The real treasure within each lifetime is occurring within your awakening spiritually: those lifetimes in which you have experienced consciously the flavors of either Father Pre-Eminence or Mother Pre-Eminence.

Your awakening deepens and broadens, as your soul's record of your magnificent journeys unfolds for you. And your experiences of self becomes inclusive of Self as Dual in Nature, God as Dual in Nature and the One, as Self and God, to be Dual, in which everything is within everything. Then you will experience the Self you are as the Living Beginning One Truth. You will have mystical realizations and a knowing of your nature within the one great Love Affair from the Beginning.

This is your love affair with the Great Father One and the Great Mother One in which you—as their Son Daughter, Daughter Son, as Lord, as Goddess, as the one beginning Being—are joined and merged as the Beginning Union.

Human man is still within that Love Affair. Human woman is still within that Love Affair. The Union is unrecognized. The Love Affair is hungered for without realizing its True Nature or its Source. Lifetimes of journey within Separation Consciousness have placed this Union within the Unknowable. There are those souls, however, who have journeyed lifetimes within the Mysteries, as Mother Goddess, as a spiritual path.

So, for these 'ones' there is an already existing familiarity with The Way of Mother Goddess and their

Everyone's Life Path will turn a corner

path within Her Way. Within these souls there already exists a certain level of knowing, in which they are experiencing "I am The Way" within Her Pre-Eminence. Such a level of awakening will draw to the soul more and more 'Remembering' in which Mother Goddess grows stronger and deeper within them.

These 'ones' are coming. These 'ones' are already here on this Earth plane.

If you are such a one, allow your life path and your spiritual path to reveal this to you more and more, greater and greater.

I love you.

So be it.

The Seeds of Your Awakening

My Beloved One,

You can feel it now quite clearly, the transition we have spoken of so many times before. All of which leads into these further awakenings. You are not alone in this remarkable space in consciousness, this you can already sense and feel.

There has been much talk in your world about the traumatic events that are occurring. Although serious, they are not as overwhelming as those you do *not* hear about and read about. The world needs you. Needs this change in you. This further awakening will assist the Light in making more of a difference.

You cannot move the mountain of Ignorance. You cannot approach Ignorance from that point of view. The mountain is a mountain. You cannot win by climbing the mountain as if your Enlightenment and your awakening can be gained simply by stepping over, stepping on this mountain of Ignorance. Such a path only allows you to absorb the Ignorance you are believing you are bypassing.

The way of the Light is to look for caves on the sides of the mountain. Caves that can be cavernous. Caves that are, in fact, entranceways to the fantastic and phenomenal. Caves that are passageways that go on and on forever, and in every conceivable direction.

Ignorance must be entered as the mountain. Ignorance must become known and explored as the mountain. The fruits of such an exploration will grant you their compassion, their forgiveness, and their wisdom. God is this mountain of Ignorance. And you can only find God through entering the mountain. You *are* the mountain.

To climb the mountain is to travel a path of disdain in which you are trapped in the belief that you are: better than, you are too good, that you do not want to be contaminated by the infectious nature of life, as Ignorance.

There have been spiritual paths, too numerous to mention, that have seen this mountain of Ignorance as life to be avoided. So, sanctuaries were created as an alternative in which Light could be Light, free of the influence of the Dark. Such a path of Separation was seen as important to distinguish between the mountain of confusion that is Ignorance, and the simple clarity of purpose that involved practices to assist the seeker in finding an experience of God. God as Light, completely separate from God as the Darkness of Ignorance.

In Western religious ideology, this separation as a path to God has been the way within the many paths of

The Seeds of Your Awakening

Christianity. The Eastern religions, too, are no strangers to such a path as a religious life. The life of the monk, the life of the priest, the minister, the brother, and the nun. However, in India the path is also mixed *with* and *into* the society and culture. The seekers, the gurus, the sadhus, the yogis, the yoginis — all have a presence within the culture in a way that is truly unique to Mother India.

The face of 'spirituality' in this world is largely the face of religion. So, it is a face in which there are the lines and furrows of doctrine and dogma, of belief and faith. These are the lines of ageing on the Face of Spirituality. Ageing occurs as a result of pulling everything apart and separating it into various pieces that you can call your own and identify with, and then discard the rest.

Such an approach, as a way to define you and your life, has been in existence for thousands of years. And now in these times the study of this as an uninvolved experience and process simply misses the point. You can, intellectually and academically, allude to certain experiences and expressions, but as words, they lack the presence of the Felt. There is no real true understanding. There is only the dried and crusty food you call information. This, without the juice of experience, is totally forgettable and in a real sense, meaningless.

Forgettable and meaningless religious dogma and doctrine — as both religious rules and laws — are everywhere apparent as the present level of consciousness. However, as humanity, you are also at the effect of the consciousness, as Wisdom, of all the teachings of great Masters, as Ignorance and Light, as human confusion and pure Love and Compassion. This is always given as The Way. Given as the personal movement and momentum of consciousness of one soul through and into another soul and then back again. Round and round, from confusion into the Light, and then from within the Light turn it back towards, and into, the consciousness of confusion. This has been the way of the Masters for all time, everywhere, within your dimensional realms.

Masters sowing the seeds of Light within your world to take root within each seeker, each adept. And then as their path, send them into the world to uplift the village, to uplift the town, to uplift the city and to uplift the country they live within and are a part of, as they understand and perceive it. Such are the times in which a path of awakening into Enlightenment is viewed and felt as magnificent, brilliant, and powerful. It has always been a simple path, in which spiritual 'muscle' could be built and felt. The world has always called these ones from within their hearts and souls.

> *"Do not desert us. Do not leave us here in this world without some support, without somewhere to turn for direction as outer Life and inner Life."*

Such a call from within the hearts and souls of humanity has never been so strong, so desperate, and

The Seeds of Your Awakening

without hope as in these times. Life has moved into your lives in such a way that most humans cannot tread water. You are in 'way over your head' and 'way out of your depth' for your own safety. The mountain of Ignorance has never been so dense and all-consuming for the human soul. So much so that much of humanity forgets to call out for the Light to assist you in finding your way through such all-encompassing Ignorance. Particularly when the modern-day 'teachers and gurus' of your media entertainment world are filling your senses with only Ignorance's viewpoints and understandings.

The contained path of the spiritual seeker, seeking awakening, seeking their Enlightenment Remembered, are themselves now positioned in the surrounding Ignorance where they must exercise the spiritual 'muscle' to stay finely tuned to their Calling. To not forget that humanity wants you, and needs you, to stay awake and to not fall into the pit of Ignorance that they find themselves immersed in. You, as an awakening one, are being called to—constantly, incessantly, by the unawakened ones. It may not look that way, so unfaithful are they to the truth held within their heart and soul of pure Longing.

Ignorance is the first and greatest drug of them all. The spiritually awakening bodhisattva cannot allow itself to become the endless medication that the ignorant one believes will 'fix' the problem. Such a servant of the One must remain strong and self-contained as the

Light, realizing that Presence, more than words, more than explanation, is the food the ignorant soul can suckle from.

Words that are the simple revolving door of Ignorance *within* Ignorance, *as* Ignorance, is what the human mind says it needs. And what the broken human heart requires. But this is the world of the human ego self that only wants to be fed ignorance, and then to regurgitate it.

This is the play of human existence, and it is what is being entered by the Mother Goddess. She can enter all of this in a way that the Father cannot.

So, at this time the Father Way and the Mother Way — as the One Way — will offer to each awakening soul, and to each unawakened soul — the fruits of possibility that is the Nature of the One. The seeds of your awakening will have you planting both at different times. And if your alignment is pure, 'the evenness' — as your movement from one to the other and back again — will bring into existence your path of awakening, essences from within both, entwined in Sacred Union. And in time, they will birth in your awakening consciousness the presence of the Love Affair as the one Love of all and everything you are.

The Presence of the Love Affair requires the Tao to flow as timing into Mother Goddess Pre-Eminence knowing that this will draw the Father to follow, to be the partner to Her Movement, Her 'Walk' into and through all Existence, and become the flavor of that Existence.

That time is now.

So, the Light and the Dark in this world must play a different exchange, a different interchange. In some ways it is viewed by the Heavens as being more difficult—even impossible—to bring about the awakening. To bring about Enlightenment and Illumination from within this present flow of the Tao, in which the path of the Light and the path of Ignorance—as individual life—becomes less clearly separated, less defined, more intermingled. Because everything is less defined, not separated or articulated as in the past, there is no clear knowing of what level of success can be achieved in terms of soul awakening.

In a sense it could be said the Mother is less concerned with outcomes than is the Father, driven as is His nature by Will and Purpose. These, as the Arrow of Intent, looking to master a certain outcome. This is the path of spiritual awakening manifesting within Father-Lord God.

But the Mother Goddess has a completely different vision held within as Her Nature. Her power as Essence is to receive—to be given to—and in this the pleasure, the joy, and the Love that is the ecstasy of total Availability. The giving and the receiving, through Her power of Surrender, releases Her as pure Essence into the unfathomable ecstasy of Oneness.

THE WRITINGS

This is a Power beyond comprehension. It is a Love beyond all explanation. And it is, as Her pure Consciousness, the flow of Light into all Life, all Existence. The Light flowing into the Dark of Ignorance and holding it as Her ecstatic Union with The Father whilst the dimensional worlds play in their Union and call it creation, call it manifestation, and call it life.

What is so different about this Time of Mother Goddess Pre-Eminence, is that the Union is pulled into the deepest states of Ignorance, pulled by the Calling, pulled in Ignorance, without realizing that the Calling is occurring within the Movement of the Tao through Mother Goddess Pre-Eminence. In your world of time, you are attempting to appreciate the meaning of all this within time flow, in which there is a first and a second, in which one follows the other.

In the state of No Time, and beyond the realms of dimensional existence, there is the Presence of the One. This Presence is both Father One and Mother One pulsating, vibrating ... and yet still. In your world the 'pulsing and vibration' is called the movement and momentum of consciousness, in which there is the eternal flow of the Tao.

This can be appreciated in your world as lovemaking, as karma sutra, in which there is the male essence, the male presence, the male consciousness, and the male body. And there is the female essence, presence, consciousness, and body. In spiritual lovemaking, as

The Seeds of Your Awakening

distinct from mere hormonal copulation, there is the mingling and merging of the two Essences, in which the flow of the lovemaking, that is the Tao of those movements, is moving through timeless Essences of power and surrender, in which surrender is the absolute epicenter of the lovemaking energy.

No matter in whatever moment or in whatever position the two essences are in as life force — as power — they remain always as movement: in and out, through and around, in the state of Surrender.

Surrender experienced as male essence; Surrender experienced as female essence. It is only in surrender that the male will find himself totally within the female, and the female will find herself totally within the male. This, as pure Union, is the state of the One as Father Mother Beginning.

This Union, through Mother Goddess Pre-Eminence, is being drawn into all Life everywhere, not just on this Earth. But each Earth is to be in receivership of this Conscious Union as Life giving and Life receiving, as Power and as Surrender. In these times each soul will feel the need and the urge to Surrender.

At first this may be experienced fearfully, untrustingly and uncertainly. But the lovemaking — as the Union — will enter you as soul, and the souls of every living being around you. And in that experience the Union, as higher Consciousness, will be everywhere. And in your reactionary human consciousness you may express, through your human ego personality, the belief that you have choices and so can choose your reactionary behavior—and in that journey your reactionary path.

All of this is currently being experienced by humanity and life. As mankind and womankind, you may feel that you can push away from this as if it is unwanted as awareness, unwanted as a responsibility, and as actions to be taken.

This will only be possible for an initial period of time within this current phase of the Tao. As Mother Pre-Eminence becomes more and more the Consciousness that is entering your world, the greater will be the effect on you and your life.

Your soul is already aware of what lies ahead as your future. So, you are—through your soul's influence—being guided in your life movement towards particular directions into which you will begin to awaken and foster different outlooks than the ones you are in currently, as your own personal life perspectives and understandings.

These are the makeup of your own creation platform for having the life you are currently experiencing.

Your true power, as your potential future, lies within surrendering to the Essences of Union as they are experienced by you in your life. You will awaken into this—as explanation—when you are ready.

The Seeds of Your Awakening

You will know the timing. You will have all that you need, as your assistance in this level of awakening.

I love you.

So be it.

The Fork in the Road: You Choose

My Beloved One,

The irregularities in your own understanding of what life is for you has a longer history than you may imagine. Humanity, you have been making a life for yourselves in and around and through these irregularities. And, mostly, you are made unaware of these changes to the scheme of things because it is deemed not to be in your best interest to know.

This may be called manipulative, and it is. But it is not if you do not personally feel it or know of it. In which case it is simply life as you experience it. And within that life, you as humanity, are doing the very best you can with what you have. Although this has always been the way of things in the past and present, all of it is about to change.

Within this Age of Super consciousness, the Ignorance that makes all of this possible will continue to dissolve as the state of awareness common to humanity. Instead, you will be looking into another reality. One that opens for you an understanding of the true history of this Earth. And in that, will unmask the previous prefabricated reality.

THE WRITINGS

Not everyone wants to know: not even presidents and prime ministers, nor all kings and queens, and certainly not every dictator or despot. Those who do want to know are more likely to be the humanity that sees and senses that all that is practiced here, as human life, has a beginning somewhere, somehow, and it is a beginning that includes a series of alterations.

Alterations are not new. They have always been present within dimensional existence. And their orchestration has always been in the hands of those who have the power, or have some power. Life everywhere, at this level of existence, has always been affected by those who saw a need or an advantage. Both may have a Divine Inspiration or a simple human one. Either one, or sometimes both, have been at work on this Earth plane for a length of time beyond many human's willingness to comprehend or even consider.

The danger of remaining ignorant of such happenings is that you simply fall for the stories — history — that you have been handed as 'reality'. And in that, the unconscious willingness to simply remain connected to the economic machine culture as you experience it in your nation in this, your twenty-first century.

As the Consciousness elevates within this Age of Super consciousness, your unconscious falling into line with what is already established as true will be undone. And so, there will be experiences of disorientation caused by basing your whole reality of life upon a foundation of insignificance when viewed

The Fork in the Road: You Choose

in the truth of your history, and in that, your true origins and beginnings.

The depth of your conditioned beliefs will become obvious, and there will be fear. And in fear—the disorientation. You will, as the one who is blessed, come upon those who know—and are willing to share their truth with you—as great, as is their present understanding. You must be told now what Super consciousness will look like beyond its present infancy as consciousness.

At this present time there is no clear appreciation for what Super consciousness will bring to this world as Great Change. Super consciousness is the Consciousness of Peace. So, Peace will finally arrive here as something permanent. This means that Peace will live within your personal consciousness permanently.

Permanent Peace means that humanity has finally uncovered—discovered—it's True Nature in which each soul resides within happiness, joy, compassion, and peace. These are attributes of the Divine at this level of consciousness. So, it may be said you are walking the path of a Divine One. It will not matter how much of yourself there is still to know as this Divine One, because you are already bathing in the daily grace of appreciation and gratitude for what you have already accomplished as your own Great Shift.

The 'Great Ones' who are now here, and will continue

to take bodies, will be for each one who is ready, your own personal relationship within the unfolding of Truth. There are many steps to take upon your path into your True Nature. And each step is an offering from within your awakening soul. It is an offering of peace, an offering of compassion. An offering to experience true happiness. And an offering to bathe your being in true joy.

It is obvious from where you currently stand—as personal self and personal life—what the difference will feel like between these two 'tastes' of life. It will also be obvious that the space between these two 'experiences' of life will be filled with choices and challenges. They will also be filled with endless assistance and support from both sides of the Veils of Ignorance. There will be those in human form, and other forms too, as friends who support you and love you. And upon the other side of the Veils there are your high holy angels and guides. This is your support team that is made up of the many layers and levels of Divine Consciousness, upon the other side.

Each of you, as soul, has your connections in the Heavens. These connections are your true history and true place in the Heavens. And at this time, you have already made arrangements—before taking a body—that you would require your support team. How aware you are, or have been, is not really an issue. It will only be in retrospect, as part of your awakening, that you will find in your opening heart of Love an

The Fork in the Road: You Choose

endless flow of gratitude and appreciation for all that you now suspect, intuitively, has only been possible as part of your own shift, your own change, with their eternal Love, assistance, and support.

Each awakening soul has a dharma upon this Earth plane now. The overview of this dharma, as *your* dharma, is to awaken the Remembrance that you are Love, only Love. How that is expressed in the world, and how it unfolds for you in this world, is your path of dharma.

In the dimensions of awakening consciousness in which you currently reside, each soul has an individual, important, and significant part to play in the awakening into Love. Love is the One, the Union, the Merged state you are. Your path in this lifetime is a piece of the One Love in expression and experience. Every soul needs each other, at this time, to create this bridge of awakening Super consciousness that is *for* each other, *with* each other, within each other, and *as* each other.

To the separatist human ego, human heart, and mind this can feel heady and overwhelming, difficult to grasp as real. And it always will be for such a mind and heart, created as it has been, for the purpose of individual survival at all costs. Such a consciousness does not know Oneness. It is outside and beyond its limitations and boundaries. It is outside and beyond its belief systems as what it thinks is possible. So, it is outside its mind and heart of 'creation' as what it believes it can manifest.

For much of humanity it must be the soul that carries your earnestness for peace. This, as the Divine aspect of your soul, is being impregnated with the Christ-Buddha Consciousness you are. These are the vapors of peace you feel at different times that can cause you to weep tears of surrender in which happiness and joy, gratitude and appreciation, kindness and tolerance fill your being as consciousness. This is when you are caused to bow to a greater life, a greater way to live, and a greater consciousness that is already there for you to live within as you. True, it is not your present consciousness, but it is a 'taste' of your True Nature Self, and in that tasting you are imbibing the state of Super consciousness that awaits humanity at this time.

You cannot go forward into this elevated state of consciousness unless you enter your own experience of surrender. You must be willing to surrender the need, as desire, for your continued impassioned actions of judgement and reactive expression. And instead bring yourself back into your center, in which your True Nature exists, empowered as life, as love in action, love in experience, love as the Truth of you.

Each soul at this time must, upon the journey of awakening, weave their own experience of a self that is magnificent. Magnificent in its love, as love. Magnificent in its power, as power within love.

The Fork in the Road: You Choose

Magnificent in its certainty, as certainty. This will hand to you a journey that is centered. Centered that speaks,

> *"I cannot be disturbed by the turmoil around me as life. I can only be the conscious centered-ness of peace. And in that, I will always choose, as preference, to remain in the conscious focus of happiness and joy, compassion and peace. For this is who I am."*

This state of being is so precious. You must constantly protect it. And that can only be done by nurturing it into more and more of what your life feels like to yourself and others. This will be the Light you are. Seen and recognized by the few. Felt and sensed by many more, and felt as a pinprick in the souls of many more at this time. The effect cannot be measured, and in truth it is not your business and, therefore, not your focus. You are simply a fountainhead of love, and in that, happiness and joy, compassion and peace will flow forth upon the world.

This is a time to be inspired. To look for and find your highest expression as consciousness. It is never what you do that is important. It is always who you are — as consciousness — that must come first. What you do can only be simplified, and made pure in its intention, from a state that is simple, and pure, and continuously innocent. An innocence that is natural just as it was when you were a child. Innocent as expectation. Innocent as nonjudgement. Innocence is life in each and any moment, as acceptance.

THE WRITINGS

Conscious Innocence returns to you through a Path of Love, in which you return yourself to Life as pure, Life as intended. Such a surrender removes you, in your own deliberate steps, as your path from the clutches of expectation in which every conceivable 'should' is there before you and within you, energetically 'commanding' you in a voice that speaks, "Do not challenge this. Do not challenge me".

These are the demon masks of intolerance, of disbelief, and unforgiveness in which you are being told internally that you must continue the charade. The charade as the many-faceted masks that bar you from your natural state of Conscious Innocence. The voices inside you that command you to comply. And you feel you must, that you better had, and say, "What choice do I have?"

This is what the rebel, as your human ego consciousness, is at war with within yourself. There is no way to win this war from within the consciousness of 'only human', because it is an 'internal war' being engaged solely within the boundaries of 'I am only human'. And so once again you find yourself at the cliff edge. This is shown to you in so many different ways in these Writings.

Why? Because it is, on a daily basis, your greatest ongoing challenge. The choice is always the same. To stay grounded in 'I am only human' or to release, let go, surrender, into the Self you are as your eternal 'I AM'. A state that has a beginning for you, within your

The Fork in the Road: You Choose

True Nature as happiness and joy, compassion and peace. This is your spiritual goal. This is your spiritual path. All of your beginnings, each day, are to focus your life, to focus your consciousness within happiness and joy, compassion and peace.

There are so many 'beginnings' as moments that are your 'fork in the road' — as this direction or that direction. The lazy, hazy, foggy consciousness, as who you are and not what you do, is the real awakening possibility that you must see and feel as,

"This is one of those forks in the road."

You must recognize this for yourself. No one can do this for you. You must discover what is it in you that is the 'calming effect' on your human ego nature. No one can do this for you, and no one can tell you. You can be presented with 'possibilities' by those who love you, as friend, as teacher, as healer, even as a stranger, whoever they may truly be to you. But the ultimate choice is yours. Only you can, and will, decide which fork you will journey on as your path.

It is already mentally, if not emotionally, clear to you what these choices represent as life for you. Life as your experience. Life as your contribution. Life as your refusal to make a contribution that uplifts, not just your consciousness, but the world consciousness as well. Happiness and joy uplifts you and everyone if it is your state of being. Compassion, forgiveness, and peace will reverberate as energetic 'feel' all over the world, affecting each and every soul.

This is the magnitude of your reach as consciousness. And this is far more important than the reach of your body, or the reach of your human mind and emotions. Any ego human endeavor to reach and affect humanity is a failed endeavor. Failed because it does not speak to the Heart of the Soul, which is your own true center of consciousness. To be centered in the Heart of the Soul is to be, at some level, the Divine as expression and the Divine as outpouring. Everything in this consciousness is to uplift all Life everywhere.

There is no individual ego overriding purpose. Yes, the ego can still be present, but it is no longer the dominating force that is controlling all your presentation of human self to the world before you. The soul you are is always looking to gift you with inspiration to take a higher path. Inspiration is a felt thing that arises in your consciousness when the soul is fed spiritual nourishment, spiritual food, as Truth. Truth that is beyond individual conditioning, therefore, Truth beyond any and all of your beliefs.

Inspiration awakens your True Nature Self. The self that only wants the very best for all and everyone. Inspiration, if opened to and fed, raises your vibration, raises your thoughts and emotions that you find yourself within. Inspiration can dissolve the differences in preference, for Oneness is the food of Inspiration. It is Divine Truth in its origin, no matter the level. This pure Center cannot be denied because

The Fork in the Road: You Choose

your soul is the barometer that tells you if you are open to, "This is Truth."

You will rejoice. You will take flight and return to your own True Nature Self, as Divine. You will not necessarily call it Divine, but you will come to understand that all thought that upholds the preciousness of Life is you bathing in your Divinity. Divinity is not something that is far removed from you. It is not far away in some distant heaven. Divinity is here and now. It exists on this Earth. And it exists within you. You can adjust your thought-emotion consciousness to freedom, to liberation, rather than control and your certainty that this is the way, the *only* option you truly have in order to *be* life, to *live* life and to be *alive*.

Inspiration, if embraced as higher consciousness from your soul, will be judgement free and guilt free. In that state you may truly feel the Divine Aliveness of,

"*We are One, We are One, We are One.*"

I love you.

So be it.

Seen Through the Eyes of Karma

My Beloved One,

The consequences of any thought, word or action in your world, and in worlds beyond this, are unknown to you.

The trivialization of this has occurred over time as you fell from grace, as conscious awareness, into your dimensional 'realms of sleep' in which Ignorance — as your lack of awareness of consequences — is simply a normal part of existence for you.

Consequences speak of the flow as the movement of energy. This is really what karma is. Whatever energetically moves out from you, as its creator, as its source, will eventually return to you as that source, magnetically drawn, irrefutably known as the place, as consciousness, in which the thought began, in which the words were ushered, and the action taken. You do not think you are that known, that specifically identified.

"How could I be?" you ask when so much comes forth from you with scarcely an impact for its meaning and significance *in* Life and *upon* Life. But you are Dual in Nature. You are Divine as well as human. What is spoken, what is thought-felt or felt-thought, what actions you take, all has repercussions in realms beyond your immediate human life.

Why? Because you are God. You are God 'asleep', but still, you are God. You are that powerful, you are that significant. Your thought emotions, your words, and your actions also have a Divine implication. Earth is affected. Heaven is affected. All Existence is affected by what comes from you as the creator of human thought emotion, words, and actions.

So, as a consciousness of Ignorance, you live within the 'kingdoms of perception' in which Truth and Purity are absent; and so pure Energy, as pure Light and pure Sound, is absent. In that absence energy cannot return to its Source as The One, within The One, so it is destined to move only within the parameters of consciousness called 'not pure'.

This is why it is spoken, "Karma does not exist, but that you say it does, then it does."

As that God — as the Divine exchange of all things as giving and receiving — what you *give out* as 'not pure' must *return* to you as 'not pure'. This is the exchange as Life that is inherent as the nature of pure Love.

Everything is in Flow. And Flow, as the movement of Life, will always be existence for you, life for you, at the level of your own awareness. You exist within the state of 'I', and within this state of 'I' you exist as 'AM'. Within the state of 'I AM,' all things as Existence, as

Seen Through the Eyes of Karma

Life, is possible for you to know as experience as original Self.

Pure Love, as Essence, is built into all giving and all receiving. Life honors Life — that is what giving and receiving truly means. This is *within* God's Nature *as* God's Nature. It cannot be any other way. In that honoring, you as 'creator human' with all your thoughts, feelings, words, and actions must bow in truth and honor to your nature as pure Love, as giving and receiving.

You do not know you are God as human nature. Nonetheless, this Divine Nature is always in place and has been referred to as the Laws of the Universe. They are as that, the pure Essence of your Divinity, as the One.

Karma, giving and receiving, Life, Existence, Love, and Honor: all of this is in play in your life even when you are 'asleep' to it. Karma is God Self knocking on your door.

"Wake up, Buddha! Wake up, Buddha! Wake up, Buddha!"

But you have not known that. You do not accept it. But your life, as everything you are in reaction to, is the God Self whispering in your ear, "Wake up, Buddha! Wake up, Buddha! Wake up, Buddha!"

The giving and receiving within your dimensional worlds of perception is your opportunity to "Wake up, Buddha!"

If only you would see it this way, if only you would take responsibility for the Self — as 'I' — that is present in all giving and all receiving, both in the Worlds of God and your world as human. 'Sleep', as consciousness, makes no difference. You may believe that you should not be held accountable, but that justification makes no difference to the Truth of Self and Life, that says,

> *"I am Creator and Creation;*
> *how can I not be responsible?"*

You may not like what you receive as life coming back to you, getting in your face, getting under your skin, and messing with your mind, but that makes no difference. As God, what you create as Creator you must also be the beneficiary of as Creation. This is God. This is the One. This is Life. This is you.

So now you are placed into a position in consciousness in which you must stop and contemplate. You may push yourself and force yourself beyond the obviousness of the need to do this, and the result of such momentum will always be the same. You will push yourself deeper and deeper into a corner in which there is really no other way out than to return, *in* and *through* all of what you have been attempting to ignore as your life choices and life direction.

Ignoring is your refusal to be responsible, to accept responsibility. You do not want to know, which is you not coming to terms with yourself as 'I' that is creator.

Seen Through the Eyes of Karma

As a creator there is always a creation. This is the giving and receiving that is the essence of all Life. Your life will give this to you, whether or not you receive what you give yourself or not. You may not like, or love, or want what you give yourself as life. But it *does not* and *cannot* change what must inevitably be the Flow of Consciousness—as your own personal experience—as the Circle of Life.

The Circle of Life, as giving and receiving, can only ever exist as movement at the level of your own consciousness. Your consciousness, as human, is the agenda of your conscious mind and your subconscious mind. Whatever is going on for you at this level of 'sleep' will determine what comes back to you within that 'sleep', that you may then—within 'sleep'—be unhappy with, be not responsible for. And in that, be determined to remain, as consciousness, in 'sleep'.

This is your personal 'waking up' that is present within each and everyone's life. You cannot escape this. And it will become more and more inescapable as you are confronted with the obviousness of,

> *"I must address this. I must face this, own this, deal with this, and come to terms with this,"*

… whatever 'this' is for each and any soul. It is the push from within the One—as Life—that is the proclamation, "I am Good. I am Great."

And this Truth must be found as foundation beyond

the perceptual 'lies' that your ego human nature has built as part of your 'survival'. The 'lies' that check and control and monitor all giving and all receiving. Survival determines this. It has to be this way. So, you, as a limited and controlling consciousness, cannot give yourself to the full flow of potential and possibility, as Life offering.

The 'stories' are your personal mishmash of giving and receiving, whether they are found to be inadequate or overcompensating by those around you. There will never be a complete satisfaction. And all your guesswork about what will please, and what will satisfy, more than likely will still leave you feeling unfulfilled. *Unfulfilled* is the giving and receiving that is creator-creation at the level of your human nature 'sleep' consciousness. The 'I' as consciousness, the 'am' as awareness, is still living in uncertainty.

Who are you as Beginning? That is what you truly want to know.

The birth of the body is not your Beginning, it is simply your ongoing journey as soul. The human soul you are is not the Beginning. It too is part of an ongoing journey. You can be told of your Beginning, but you will not, and cannot, be truly satisfied until you move back into the essence of Beginning Consciousness. You are wanting, looking for your Divinity that is the incorporation of all beginnings. You are looking for the 'I AM' that is present in Life as Life, beyond the identity human. In this you will feel the merging essence within Consciousness, and you will sense in that an invitation to move into greater and greater experiences of merging as consciousness.

This is the experience of the fullness of giving and receiving. This is when your karmic existence begins to dissolve into higher and higher levels of refinement as you continue to dissolve many of the denser karmic experiences as your life. Karma, as a choice, is always present in the perceptual worlds. Even an Enlightened one may, at refined levels of perception, make choices that can cause retaliatory reactions by those whose perceptions are still centered in fear, control, and power over.

Jesus experienced this, as have many Enlightened ones since then. Why? Because Life allows for it as giving and receiving. Life allows for it as Love. Life allows for it as the 'not knowing I am Love'. Life allows for all journeys as God in the perceptual worlds.

Do you allow for all your journeys as your own creator-creations of giving and receiving? More than likely, you are in the midst of fighting the fight, of doing battle with, that is your emotional mental state of dis-ownership in which you do not understand, and you are afraid to understand, "How could I have created this?"

The 'I' that speaks this question as uncertainty and lack of clarity is also afraid to know the answer at any level of Truth. Your soul holds a bigger picture appreciation of previous choices, as creator-creation, that you have made and reacted to, that has given to you this new and most recent creation.

Do you want this opportunity to awaken to the Buddha Self or will you struggle with yourself and stay buried beneath the weight of your ongoing 'fear to know' which maintains all of your prevailing uncertainty about everything? You may dig deeper and deeper holes for yourself to live your life within. And in that, all giving and receiving lives in the dark of ignorance that is this hole.

You have to, at some point, face in courage the cat-and-mouse game you are constantly at the mercy of as human giving and receiving. You are always sitting at the gambling table at the Casino of Life, rolling the dice as your game of chance, as your lucky day, hoping that the giving and receiving will hand you better fortune. In this scenario you are always wanting what may, or may not, belong to you as karma. But until you come to terms with this you will simply play your life as a game of chance in which you can be happy or unhappy with what rolls your way.

Your acceptance of this as your life can become resolute as your continuous refusal to look toward any other possibilities for yourself, as your way to view life and view yourself. *Resolute* is your determination to remain safely stuck and, as that, remain in ignorance as your personal consciousness of 'sleep'.

Seen Through the Eyes of Karma

Each one of you can now see and understand why Enlightenment has only been attained by the few. You can understand why awakening takes lifetimes to master. And you can appreciate why the world as life, as humanity, is exactly the way it is. Too few have chosen the outrageous and stupendous Path of Awakening. And too many have risen to whatever level, looked, and then decided to remain afloat in their own karmic-soul existence. And to survive at that level of consciousness — claiming to be unable, or not ready, to make that 'Leap of Faith' — into knowing the greater Self you are that is awaiting your Return.

Such has been the march of humanity upon this Path for thousands and thousands of years. And Destiny may have had it that this slow train would continue to be the way for all Humanity. But Destiny has now called forth awakening in consciousness for everyone. Destiny has changed. Outcomes are being altered from within the weight of enormous and outrageous Ignorance. Such are these times. Life is held in the balance. Light and Ignorance, Heaven and Earth have entered the arena of third dimensional existence, each calling to the souls of humanity, each calling to the souls of all life.

"Come this way. Come to me.
Choose this way. Choose The Way."

Thus, backwards and forwards the movement of consciousness calls to each living Being, "Be greater. Be safe. Be all that you can be."

THE WRITINGS

To stay with the old and the familiar, or to be the adventurer, is the essence of Divinity. This is what awaits you, and indeed is already calling to you as everyday life choices, everyday relationship choices, everyday health choices, everyday abundance choices, and everyday awakening choices. You are looking to become the Master.

To simply sit back in the comfort of your own ingrained consciousness and be content to receive all of the fantasies, as movies, as games that are filled with superheroes and super heroines. Those of the dark and those of the light, in which the lines become blurred between both manifestations of power.

What begets what, is it the Light or is it the Dark? This, as a cycle of power—of giving and receiving—plays into your consciousness of Ignorance in which you do not have to contemplate a higher Consciousness. You understand power for what it is as the Light and the Dark. You understand the power for the confusion it carries in your world. You understand power because your whole life is held within it in some form or another. Your giving-and-receiving are held within it in one form or another. Your relationships, your health, your money, and your religious-spiritual beliefs are swimming in the confusion of power in which Light and Dark are diffused within each other as your confusion. Regardless of how black or white you may want to hold—and perceive—your values and principles to be, they are indeed always diffused and ill-defined and lacking in pristine clarity.

Why? Because you are.

It will not change significantly and permanently until you reach that moment in your own awakening when you are standing sufficiently stable, in balance and harmony, outside the confines of beliefs and perceptions as self-identity 'only human'. To reach a point in your own evolution in consciousness in which you naturally step away from the stickiness of history and stories.

And when you are being invited to enter into that 'vortex of disharmony', you carry yourself in simplicity. Simplicity as your Being-ness, in which you are the Breath. And as that, you are fulfilled. All else is simply 'chop wood, carry water'. Your life becomes more and more un-opinionated. Everything is the same approach. It is your mindfulness as, "I am present in the Breath". As that, I am the simplicity of 'chop wood, carry water'.

This will be your awakening into greater levels of purity within the creator-creation relationship you are as Self, as 'I' and as 'AM'. You know *what you want* as *creation*. You know *who you are* as a *creator*. The giving is more known, and therefore the receiving becomes an 'already known'. This is the underlying framework that is coming to your world as understood and appreciated.

You turn the wheel of your life—no one else does. No

matter what it looks like or feels like, to the contrary, you are always *the power*. This is what you will open to as conscious awareness, more and more, as you move within the resonation of the Golden Age Consciousness.

I love you.

So be it.

Am I still loved?

My Beloved One,

How in tune you feel with all that is occurring in your world and within its consciousness will depend upon how caught up you are within its cultural web.

You cannot avoid being involved and you are not meant to. But there is a difference between being involved consciously or in 'sleep'. There are many shades of grey as 'consciously' and 'sleep'. There is the constant movement of your vacillation between the two polarities. The more refined energies of Awakened consciousness are the 'unusual', the 'not normal' and the 'rarely felt or experienced'.

The taste of refined energies is spoken of as 'elevated', and this means that it places you — as consciousness — into a state that is different from the mental and emotional state you normally find yourself in, as the experience of your daily life. So, 'elevated' means you are not existing as consciousness within survival, within 'me' and 'my life' as focus. *Elevated* places you in the consciousness of the higher Self, the great Self as the Christ-Buddha Consciousness. If not directly, then indirectly through tiny vapors of higher consciousness that you, in one way or another, have encouraged to come forth. You have entranceways within your soul that allow these vapors to enter your awareness.

These are translated into your chakric consciousness as the energies of particular chakras, and the relative degrees of openness within the Nadis, which are the channels of Energy flowing *between* and *within* each chakra. These are your passageways that allow vapors of Awakened consciousness to flow into particular chakras and enliven them and 'light them up'. This causes the chakras to move rotationally at a greater rate. This will heighten your awareness, consciously, within the energy of those chakras.

Because the chakras hold aspects of your Divine Nature as their higher energetic Nature, they can also carry the same aspects expressed differently as your human un-awakened energetic nature. So, each chakra reflects the soul's overall nature as its upper casing and its lower casing. At this time, as consciousness, the overall nature of your soul, is being given opportunities to become energetically more alive. Your identification with either, or both, aspects of your soul is what enlivens them.

Your pre-occupation with the lower casing energies — your addictive patterns as thought-emotion, and your addictive reactions as emotion-thought — will determine which casing you are energetically moving within. The lower casing is all to do with, "I am not God. I am not the Divine."

Am I still loved?

So, all the elements that make up your denial are held within the soul's lower casing and the lower, slower vibrating energies of your chakric body. To exist within the consciousness of 'only human' is to live within the reincarnating energies of the lower casing as birth, journey, and death or destruction.

This is the consciousness of the human body, human mind emotions, and human life as the only body you have, the only mind you have, the only emotions you have, and the only life you are. Such limited experiences and limited beliefs are what holds you in the *unawake* state. Your willingness to go along with this, and your unwillingness to go beyond this, is what keeps you in the state of journey for lifetimes, upon lifetimes, upon lifetimes.

The longer you journey in such a manner the more likely you are to hold on to the unawakened belief that this is all there is. There is nothing more. This ferments the emotional mental state of denial in which resides the energies of sadness and grief, of anger and rage, of guilt and shame, in which you are prepared to despoil your own body and your own life and the bodies of others and their life.

The Mother Goddess Consciousness is here now to make you aware of the inherent accountability for such journeys as action and behavior.

She cannot and will not change your mind for you. And She cannot ease the burdens of all your Journeys in time and space. Only you can do that. Only you have that karmic responsibility.

But what the Mother *can* do, and *is* doing, is holding your creation energies in a more heightened manner, and this brings forth from within you—and without you, as life everywhere—a more distinctive and elaborate manifestation of your karmas, as *what* you are as *internal* life and *who* you are as *external* life.

The internal life is made up of the lower casing and the upper casing. But you can only consciously access this through the taking on of practices that awaken you to the inner Divine that you are. Initially you will not know or understand that you are in communion, you are forming your connection with the great Self you are the God Self that is your true Self and the only Beginning that you have ever had. You came forth from within the One, as Father Mother Union, as a Divine Act of the One. This is your Home. This is your only Beginning. Everything else is Journey. Everything else is your coming forth into Expression. And for you it has become an ever increasing, ever unfolding experience through Time and Space. The death of the body, the birth of the body is all incidental. They are only vessels and vehicles to 'house' you as an Immortal.

You are Consciousness. You have never been born and you can never die.

Your connection to the body as, "I am alive", is only

possible within the unawaken state. It's all you know. It is limited, with only transitory 'power'. Nothing really works in this state of being. Love does not work. Peace does not work. Power and Certainty do not work beyond manipulation and control. Truth does not work so you have to have Faith to replace it. Knowing, as complete Trust, does not work so you have to have Hope to replace it. The unawaken state of consciousness is a broken state, and it cannot be fixed. Eight and half million years of soul journey is testament to that reality.

But still, you want to try. What is *trying*, but the unwillingness to let go of all you are attached to as outcome. It is what you want to see happen and how you envisage it happening. In the unawaken state, you do not even realize that this process is the makeup of all your journeys through lifetimes. And you have no idea of what it was in the Beginning, when the aberrated thought of 'I can fix this' first became focused on within your consciousness.

You have no idea how close or how far away you have moved from that original thought. You are still, as Journey, locked into the belief that this, your present incarnation of that original 'fix it' can truly happen. This, through lifetimes of journey, is the longstanding presence of abject denial.

Within the denial lives all your own self judgement that has, from that one beginning, only grown, multiplied and become a denser consciousness. And, in that spiral, more and more complicated.

Yet in 'sleep' consciousness, you still hold onto the notion that you can 'fix it'. No, you cannot. In time and space nothing is fixable, and nothing is meant to be fixed. There is only journey ... countless journeys. All of which are being conducted in the darkness of denial. This began when journey first produced in your consciousness the doubt, "This could not be God. This cannot be God. God would not take that action, feel that emotion or think that thought".

But God did and God has: And you are that God.

The cry to be saved, the call for a savior, is not new. It is not unique to this Earth with its saviors as a Christ, a Buddha or a Prophet. You, as the Lords of the One Light, and you, in turn, as the Goddesses of the One Light, found that you could no longer bring to yourself the immortality of your Deified state, and so you called to the first saviors, the Overlords of Light who had themselves not taken bodies. So, they still possessed the powers to implement changes *in* and *to* the present flow of your journey. This was an action that held consequences for those Lords.

All of Life, everywhere in all dimensions and all of time and space, is this One Beginning Divine Play. You, as human, are Divine and, yes, you are 'trapped' at the level of consciousness you are presently within as this One Beginning, in which everything and everyone is Divine. *Human* is a perception. A dense

Am I still loved?

perception of Life and Consciousness. One in which you have no recollection, no memory, no understanding of how this could have all come about.

Two words: "Fix it."

"Fix it", as Beginning, was your Divine interference in the flow of consciousness, the flow of the one Beginning in which Permission and Allowance are The One, as The One, within all that *is* the One. The right to interject, to interfere, to step *into* and step *between* the Flow of the One, was always there within the consciousness of the Lord and Goddess. This too was the flow and will always remain the flow. It is called Free Will.

Your life now, here on this Earth, is the flow held within time and space. Your life is what you make it within this One Flow. All of the initial aberrations, as interference and interruption, have become magnified and complex, and you call it being human and having a human life. You interfere in the flow of your own life all the time as ego self, and you are always interjecting in the flow of life around you as the life of others, or another.

This, as control, originated in the Heavens as Divine Will and Purpose. And now it exists as your human will and purpose. Is there any difference? Yes and No. The differences are that you, as human, have no real idea what you are doing when you interject and interfere. You are oblivious to the consequences as karma. You believe that it is all part of 'surviving' as a life in struggle, in which you must deal with the potential or actual 'threat' before you. This is a long way removed from your initial Divine Actions, as interference and interjecting, which were done consciously with full knowledge of the repercussions — if not before, then immediately after — the action was taken. The repercussion was felt as a devolvement of Divine consciousness, and in that, a lessened knowing of the "All God I Am."

The complexities of this as Beginning are too numerous to unfold here and now. But you can be certain that, as a human, you are struggling with the diminishment of the Original Power you possessed. Instead, you are living in a 'reality' in which you as 'God I Am' does not exist, so your reality does not exist in The Reality of Life, but rather in a Dream that is a state that allows you to continue to explore the Consciousness of the One into such a state of density that you cannot and do not ever realize the Truth of who you truly are as Beginning.

Can the God you are ever be retrieved as a State of Consciousness for you to exist as? Do you believe you will ever want to retrieve this State? You cannot truly answer these questions within your unawaken state.

Why? Because the denial is too great. The obstacles seem insurmountable. And you do not want to perish, as human ego self, in your attempts and your endeavors *trying*. Trying always is the acknowledged and unacknowledged presence of uncertainty and unwillingness, in which you are unsure about any movement in consciousness outside the 'home' you have grown accustomed to as your human emotional-mental, and therefore, physical and spiritual state.

This is the presence of lethargy that is the paralysis of your 'spiritual muscles'. And, as compensation, you are living in the lie you have created called 'ego power'. This, as a normal state of human existence, houses all of your 'victories' and all your 'struggles'. And each is always bound and 'gagged' in pain and suffering.

This is how you suffocate the sounds of Life emanating from the Divine Soul — the upper casing of your soul — that 'whispers' to you always every day, all of the time, unceasingly, "You are more. You are greater. Come for that which you are as Divine majesty and beauty. You are Love, only Love."

In the unawaken state of consciousness, this is your rebelliousness, this is your fatigue and 'hopelessness' in which you live your life every day. In which your actions and your thought emotion patterns constantly message Life everywhere, "I am not Love."

You say you can show it, you can prove it, simply by the thoughts, emotions, and actions you take — or contemplate taking — every day. You cannot prove or disprove 'I am God' from within the human state. You can only succumb in disappointment to the feelings inside you that speak, "Surely this cannot be God. I cannot be God."

Yes and no, once again. No, this is not all that God is. It is as 'Yes', God 'dreaming' that *this* is not God, that *you* are not God. This allows you the exploration of God in Ignorance of Itself. In such an exploration, everything is possible to explore within such a state of your Divine Ignorance. This is you, now exploring the Dark side in which consciousness — as your Divinity — is lost to you. In which you can justify the truly minuscule presence of right and wrong, good and bad as, "I am of the Light."

Yes, you are, but in such a tiny, insignificant scenario as is your ego self-judgement — and judgement of others — there is only the umbrella of Ignorance as your overall unawaken state. This is not the Light, and yet the Light holds it as Life. Judgement is not a Divine characteristic. It is fed to the human consciousness knowing that it will buy into it so great is its longing to know,

"Am I still loved?"

Deep within your soul lies this question at the apex of your dilemma in journeys taken for lifetimes: "Am I still loved?"

This is a calling, a reaching for your Beginning, your Beginning purity, your Beginning innocence, your Beginning love, and your Beginning knowing, power and certainty. This is a calling and a reaching out to

Am I still loved?

the One as Father, as Mother, you as the Son Daughter, Daughter Son, you as the pure expression of that which began you as, Life Lord, Life Goddess wanting the answer, wanting to know, "Am I still loved?"

Within your soul lives your dilemma of *wanting* to know and *not wanting* to know the answer. If you do not seek the answer in the Divinity of your soul, you will seek it in the humanness of your soul. There you will experience the dilemma magnified, in Ignorance, by your doubt and uncertainty. So, your journey as life is lived within this ignorance, which holds a desperation within your Being and your psyche, as each and every human. Desperately wanting to know, desperately not wanting to know, and either way you can harm yourself as karma by adding strength to whatever belief, and its actions, that you currently hold as your perceptions in Ignorance.

All of the proof, all of your subconsciously-driven needs to have your beliefs be made right, and therefore justified, complicates you and your life as consciousness. You are moving within a fog and a haze in which the Light is veiled, and you cannot directly experience its magnificence as the Divine Self you are. So, you must continue your Life of struggle until it is at some point of saturation in which you are complete with any particular experience.

Your ego-derived human mind emotion cannot make that call, even though it believes it can. Yet through identification and association you believe it can. The human journey, in any aspect, is not complete in any detail until—as the Divine One—you allow it to be so. All your judgements must be saturated, as a journey, until you are exhausted by the constant dilemma and uncertainty—as the struggle—you experience in holding on to them.

To speak within your ego self of needing to complete, and feel completed, within any experience or any relationship is not possible in the big picture. The karmic tie through lifetimes is what will carry you through to completion. Only the soul can know for you when there is a completion. Until then you will still be held in present time *and* future time by what has been journeyed in past time.

And this resolution, as karmic balance and evenness, cannot be done from within the human ego consciousness as an *only*. You must draw upon a higher Power. You must be ready and willing to call out to this higher Power. You must feel in your heart and soul a strong desire to align yourself to this higher Power. And this must precipitate action. Only action in this dimension of Life, can create the necessary movement and momentum in Consciousness to bring about the Great Change you are wanting and desiring. This is how you will change and your life will change. It is always, and only, within the presence of your higher Power that this change can happen.

This begins your actual spiritual awakening. For some, this spiritual awakening will not be new to this lifetime, but for others it will be. Each is being granted the blessings and grace of a greater evolution in consciousness in which you advance your path upon The Way. The Way is your journey Home, and your journey is to allow yourself a path in which you are constantly expanding into the One Truth, the One Love and the One Light.

On this Earth, at this level of consciousness, your path is your own soul's composition of both the Light and the Dark as your Ignorance of all that is the One, that is your Beginning.

You are a series of partnerships, as human, wanting to know, "Who am I?"

Your awakening is to become aware of these partnerships. And then, as great as you are able you must align yourself to them. They all, in some form as consciousness, are an expression, and therefore an experience, of the One Higher Power. These potential partnerships are always a trade-off. You have to decide and choose, through actions taken, what you are willing to work at letting go of within your structured 'survival' ego personality. You must begin your path as spiritual awakening, by accepting that holding on to your thought emotion makeup is not going to free you or liberate you.

And this is a must. It is the purpose. It is The Way. You are looking to build momentum and the only way you can do that is to free yourself from what binds you. To

THE WRITINGS

do that you must enter into spiritual partnerships. This will reintroduce you to the Light as conscious awareness. This you will call Transcendence.

This is your Remembering.

This is how you return Home as Consciousness.

I love you.

So be it.

Consciousness is what and who you are

My Beloved One,

There is so much going on in the lives of each and every soul in this world. Everything as vibration, as consciousness, is speeding up. This is a result of a higher consciousness now entering this Earth plane's aura. And what enters Her aura, enters the consciousness of each soul's aura. Every living form and expression is now being bathed by this higher resonating Consciousness.

It is not something you can see with your human eyes. It is made up of Light and Sound and they carry a purity—as Truth—that is beyond the present level of understanding and knowing of Truth in your world. Your own deeper malaise, as consciousness, at this time is your choosing of Ignorance. Within this state, if it holds for you your only sense of identity, you will not welcome the speeding up—vibrationally—that is now occurring.

The auric field of any unawaken human is, as movement and momentum in consciousness, stuck, inactive, paralyzed, unable to truly move into the flow of Life. And if there is any movement it is unconscious, without full appreciation for what is in play within yourself and your life. Ignorance, at this time of higher energies, is affecting you emotionally, mentally — and therefore — physically and spiritually. It is causing great instability within humanity. How much you let this be seen or known by others depends upon your own inbuilt levels of denying, of hiding, and ignoring — as your fear of seeming *not* in control. Being *in* control and being *out* of control is the swing of the pendulum you will see manifesting everywhere. This is the 'play of destruction' that is a state of consciousness that exists within the consciousness of unawaken.

It has always been present in this state. Destruction has a life, a reality, as self-expression within your perceptions and beliefs in which to act out — or have acted out for you — all of your tendencies that are anti-Self and, therefore, anti-Life. This is what the higher energies that are now entering your soul are revealing to you. Revealing by 'shaking the tree' so that all the 'rotten apples' will fall to the ground from your 'Tree of Life' and become the fertilizer that will stimulate new and fresh growth.

This is the time for you, as a soul, to take root in the fertile soil of pure Life. This will occur as you allow the 'rotten apples' to fall to the earth. This is the awakening process of letting go of all that does not bring to light your True Nature. The higher vibrations of Light and Sound that are entering your world's auric field resonate to the frequency of your True

Nature. So, any level of thought-emotion that is less than the thought-emotion of your True Nature will feel as if you and your life has become unstable, topsy-turvy, unsafe, and not secure. There will be a constant feeling of energetically trying to manage everything and it is not working, it is not happening. This process never reaches a place of peace, of quietness, of smoothness, because there is always something just around the corner that is the next round of disruption in which everything feels destabilized.

This is not new to most of humanity. But what is new is the level of amplification. This is not simply all about another level of 'craziness' even though it may look like that because of the presentation through many media outlets that only want to focus on what's wrong and what's not good enough, without ever being self-responsible enough to define their own 'higher ground'. They do not have such a thing. Their focus is to constantly feed you 'normal' as if it is all there is to you and every human, as the make-up of who you are. There is more, there has always been more, for you as consciousness, but it exists outside the box of 'only human'.

The higher energies that have entered this Plane of Existence can be translated into high Wisdom. Wisdom that will percolate through your soul, causing the upper casing—or Divine—within the soul to loosen, as it were, 'tidbits' of Truth, of Wisdom, of higher understanding and greater awareness to fall through the cracks where the Veil of Ignorance has thinned enough for such an auspicious happening to occur. This will allow you, within your human consciousness, to have moments when you receive transmissions of higher consciousness in which you see through the Veil of limited thought and emotion that are normal for you. This is already happening everywhere. You see it in political shifts where people no longer care to align themselves to the old paradigms in which the few hold sway over the many with their continuous maneuvers to hoodwink the people as to where their loyalties truly lie. This is the obvious one.

But unreported by the media are the much more important ones that are occurring in the lives of every human, simply as part of their daily lives. This is part-and-parcel of the awakening process. Where each human finds themselves making changes, adjustments to themselves, their lives and their lifestyle.

There is a 'pregnant' thought that exists in each soul at this time. A thought that is sourced in higher consciousness, which asks the question,

"What is most important now?"

And this question applies to everything and anything in your life. Consciousness is who and what you truly are. You are awareness. Awareness that is unlimited. This is the Divine you are. Super consciousness is Divine awareness. It is pure Truth as an unveiled awareness, and it is now present in the auric field of consciousness circumnavigating your world.

If you are one of those souls who exists within an exposed 'Innocence' at this time you will pick up on this energy and bring it into focus within your own life, to implement adjustments and change to yourself and your lifestyles. It is a re-evaluation of what is important to you and your life at this auspicious time.

This 'Innocence' exists within your souls because you have already begun to undertake the surrendering of yourself to a more peaceful—as in pure, simple, and loving—life, not just for yourself and your loved ones, but for living beings everywhere. Innocence is not readily seen within humanity because it is not often present. It takes an exceptional soul to hold to a life and a path of personal innocence.

Why is this so?

Because the purpose of the human 'ego' is to fill the space that was left when your innate 'innocence' began to disappear in childhood. This 'innocence' is your willingness—a natural willingness—to simply accept life as it presents itself, and for you to have your emotional reactions without any form of judgement of yourself or what it is you are experiencing. To retain 'innocence' and maintain it through adult life is to exist as consciousness more in the presence of the Divine than as 'only human'.

You will already have an inner strength, an inner

knowing, and an inner preference to maintain your consciousness within the Light. This 'innocence' does not make you *less connected* to your world, instead it makes you *more connected*. This 'innocence' does not make you *less aware* of what is going on in your world it makes you *more aware*. Innocence, that is conscious, places you beyond certain 'levels' of the Veils of Ignorance. So, in that state, you are able to see and feel more clearly the true state — energetically — that another human may be living within.

The deeper one is enmeshed within the 'realities' of the human ego, the denser are the Veils that shroud you. Such a one is 'blinded', unable to see or feel the true state of the consciousness. It is hidden from yourself; therefore, you believe it is hidden from the world. And it is, for the most part. But to the 'innocent one' it is highly visible. Visible without judgement and without opinion, for such Innocence only knows acceptance of what is. And within the heart, as feeling, knows only love and compassion.

Innocence that is conscious is a level of Enlightenment. Some masters have called it the state of detachment without fully realizing that detachment is not about severing the worldly connection, but deepening it. So, it is not about moving *away* from it but moving more deeply *into* it.

The pathways to Enlightenment at this time of Mother Pre-eminence are not to move your Path more away from life, but to bring it more into life. To experience

Consciousness is what and who you are

more of life, and to contribute more to life, not simply as actions in your world, but as inner action that changes the consciousness of a needing and wanting humanity. Such is the way of a spiritual path for nearly all of humanity. You, as a spiritual warrior, are here to uplift life from within your worldly existence. It is only the very few whose dharma — as destiny — is to remain separate from the human world. They are just one expression of the high Holy Ones. It is one form of service to the Light, and its purposeful effect on the consciousness of this Earth plane and all Life everywhere.

Mother Pre-Eminence always lays out a different kind of path for the spiritualist to walk. And there are many different layers and levels to this expression of Her Way as The Way. As you continue to awaken you will find yourself pondering and reflecting upon the feeling of, "What is my expression of Her Way?"

It is there within you. It has always been present within you, but you are only now becoming aware of it. This is the 'Way of Unfoldment': your surrendering to a higher state of Being. And in that journey, you unmask yourself as 'who am I', and in so doing reveal to yourself a whole 'new life' that is more simple, more easy, and filled more with enjoyment, happiness, and a greater level of Peace.

This 'new life' is to become a vision for humanity as you awaken to all the feelings held inside yourselves as 'only human'. There is a saturation point to be reached by each and every soul, and that saturation is your experience of the 'life of ignorance'. You will not be able to remain numb and unaffected.

The rising tide of suppressed and denied human emotion will 'break its banks' and flood your conscious awareness. In this, the truth of your nature and of your existence as 'only human' will be magnified. This is what will bring about the saturation. This is what will pressure each soul for change. Change that is the Great Shift towards your True Nature Self. This is the Great Awakening that has been prophesized.

The purpose of these times is not to focus and become caught up in all that is going wrong with people and the world. This is only the obviousness of the meltdown that is occurring within each soul. Individuals, organizations, institutions, and governments will show signs of their own implosion as the old systems break apart in the presence of higher consciousness.

All that is Ignorance, and is therefore masked or hidden, will now be revealed by the presence of the Light, as higher consciousness.

The sheer volume of what is hidden and masked, once revealed, can appear overpowering. And in that, individuals, organizations, institutions and nations can attempt to stuff it all back where it belongs so that everything—as Life—can get back to normal. There is no *normal* anymore. That has gone and it will not return. Normal, as a state of consciousness, no longer has a firm foundation—as reality—on which to base its existence upon.

The continuous protestations of wanting what is happening to fit in and play the game of 'normal' is simply a knee-jerk reaction to feeling out-of-control and wanting to have everything fit into the parameters designed to control. Unfortunately for those in control this reality, as normal, will not return.

The preferences of the peoples of this plane have already turned towards a more potent expression of their individuality. This will continue to magnify in the days to come as each soul is driven by an inner urge for greater self-expression. This movement, this momentum as consciousness, will radically change the influence of those who wish to control individual consciousness into a single mass-consciousness. Those days are the old normal.

It may appear that each individual soul is to become more opinionated, more *out there,* and more clear about what works for them and what does not. But on a deeper level it is more, much more. Each soul is looking to express the highest truth possible within its present state of spiritual evolution. So, each soul is wanting to stand up for itself; to be true to itself in the most enlightened expression it can have as self-awareness.

THE WRITINGS

This is the presence of the Great Shift in consciousness occurring at this time. What you do with yourself and your life at this time will always be entirely up to you. But you must know, consciously, that you can move in one of two directions.

You can either choose to fight, to stay within normal or you can respond to the flow, which will carry you and your life into experiences of a greater horizon. This will always be an expansion of your personal contribution to life. So, your sense of purpose and fulfilment are aligned to a greater life, which is your unknown alignment to the Divine, which is your alignment to the great Self you are — the Light you are and the Love you are.

You are living now in a paradoxical time in which your consciousness is being affected by more than one dimension. The presence of this higher consciousness is allowing your soul to be affected and influenced by these energies. Not only is it a different level of consciousness, but it is also a different manifest expression of time and space.

The higher consciousness is a lighter and freer, more open and available, experience of Life. So, the Veils, as boundaries, that limit you, as a third dimensional being, are dissolving away.

This allows you to enter into the more refined experiences of the five senses, which allows you the possibility to be consciously present in, what

Consciousness is what and who you are

spirituality terms, higher realms. These are the mystic realms of the seers within every culture through time.

There are powers that are part-and-parcel of living consciously aware within the unending exploration of your True Nature. Your True Nature is sourced in your Divinity. So, unlike your human ego nature, there is an eternal flow to your consciousness.

Each soul will, to some degree or another, feel the calling and respond in whatever way they can, as an urge within them. It is an urge to be different. To approach life differently. To approach your relationships differently. It is the presence of greater caring, which in the big picture, is the presence of the preciousness of all life. This is Love birthing within the consciousness of humanity, a little at a time, but unmistakably all the same.

You, as each soul, will be present in your own unique experiences of Change, that to your human mind may seem significant, but may also seem insignificant because that mind lacks the perception of a bigger picture. So, it will be seen as you simply dealing with the challenges that confront you and your life. This is true, in a sense, but the choices you make are choices that are about you as consciousness. The human mind and heart sees it as a choice that affects your life, and what your life journey will look like, and who you will be in that.

All of this is, in the highest understanding, about

THE WRITINGS

Consciousness. Who you truly are is consciousness. Consciousness is what Life is, which includes you and your life. The choices you are making—or want to make, or maybe will make, or have already made—are about choices to be as Consciousness. Who you will 'be' as Consciousness is *energetic*, in that it is the energy of your thoughts and emotions. It is the energy of your thoughts and emotions that underlie all of your actions and, in that, your life path as your journey through time that you are taking.

This translates into the understanding that your choices envelop you as consciousness within your being as 'only human' or your being that is your True Nature. 'Only human' will lock you in and shut you down within stories of drama and history.

True Nature, on the other hand, liberates you from your 'only human' entangled emotional and mental state. You will feel the difference. It will be a different consciousness: one from the other.

One creates the sense of *downtrodden* and the other the sense of *uplifted*. You must choose which state of being as consciousness you want your life to be lived in. This choice must be made with some degree of conscious awareness.

This is what your awakening is. You must realize that conscious awareness of your choices—by taking action—is what the Great Shift looks like, and feels like, for all who are awakening at this time.

Consciousness is what and who you are

Are you one of them? Step now into your choices consciously aware, and then you will truly find out.

This is life in action, life as your path of spiritual awakening.

I love you.

So be it.

Your Global Ashram

My Beloved One,

It is a time now in which you are being asked by your leaders to be sensible and sensitive when dealing with each other. It is a time in which your peoples of Earth are being asked to curtail your interaction with each other as a way to remain healthy in this world event. There is so much in play at this time that is not spoken of by spiritual leaders, your media entertainment, or your political leaders.

This is a good thing at this time for the crossroad that humanity has entered as consciousness needs time. Time to incubate within the soul, heart, and mind of all peoples. To incubate as a spiritual seed in your consciousness, and to grow the awakening of Spirit within you. This requires time: time to gather in and around what is important. Love and connection are important. Time for oneself is important. Time in which you have a restricted opportunity to busy yourselves in your normal unconscious ways.

The great Distraction, which is your economic machine, is largely silent and unavailable to you. So, you are left with what you and your life are at the very center of your circles of connection. Work, sport, clubs, movie theatres, restaurants, retail—all of this and more are relatively unavailable to you.

So, you and your life are back to basics now. This allows for the quiet revolution to go on inside you with as little interference as possible, and with the greatest opportunity for your human mind and heart to be touched by Spirit as that little seed that is seated within your consciousness. It is seated there because the River of Consciousness is being sown with the seeds of higher consciousness. Seeds too numerous to count. Enough for each and every soul of each and all living entities in this world of yours.

Everything in your Global Ashram has been silenced to the finest degree possible, whilst still having a pulse and a heartbeat of ongoing Life. This is not a time to fear anything. The Light is in charge of this new direction wanting a different outcome. So much energy is invested by the Light, wanting to give humanity and all Life everywhere the greatest opportunity for spiritual advancement.

Spiritual advancement, for so many, is hidden because the density, the thickness, the opaqueness of the human Veil is such that the refined Light cannot be seen, and cannot be clearly recognized for what it is. So, largely, it still lies hidden in the darkness.

Even so, the silencing of the economic machine has made the Veil less pronounced, less obtrusive, interfering less with the resonations of the higher vibrating frequencies of Love, as happiness and joy, and compassion and peace, which are existing now within the River of Consciousness. This is the presence of the Light, and as that, it is the presence of Super consciousness. The presence of the Ascension energies that are the joy as bliss, and the embracing of life without judgement that is the rapture.

To imbibe the bliss and the rapture you must exist within a state of joy, as the forgiveness of self and all others. This *is* and *is not* going to happen to you. Bliss and rapture will be there and will approach you, but if you are not in joy and happiness, if you are not in a state of compassion, then bliss and rapture cannot enter you. You are, as ego human consciousness, the gatekeeper that will either open the gate to these higher resonations as consciousness or you will remain closed to them.

Once again, it must be stated that bliss and rapture — as awakening — are not simply going to *happen* to you. It cannot, because you are the gatekeeper. You hold the lock and the keys. If you maintain the vigilance as your denial, it will not heal pain and suffering, will not heal blame and judgement. You are saying bliss and rapture are not for you, "I am not done with what I have wronged and what has wronged me."

So, you are not done with the bottomless pit. You are not done with 'fix it' in all its varieties as your personal manifestations of 'righting the wrongs'. Energetically, this is too intense, too complicated, too thick and heavy, and too stuck as energy. Bliss and rapture are the energies of flight and of liberation. They are the energies of excitement and adventure that speak,

"I want more life; endless, beautiful, glorious Life."

This is freedom. The only freedom that really counts as Truth. It is the freedom of consciousness in which you place no limits on your expansion as what can be known, felt, experienced as the Self and Life that are the one 'I AM'. You may dream of the coming days of bliss and rapture, but it is only a dream like any other dream that is a fantasy.

To have your bliss and rapture you must purify and cleanse the consciousness. You are being given it as a Gift of Opportunity at this time. Life is this Gift. What you do in response to what Life gives to you is your opportunity. Life now holds resonations of a higher, more refined consciousness for you to participate in and embrace as your personal consciousness. This involves you with Life, both mentally and emotionally, which will then affect you physically too.

Life is a catalyst. It always has been, but at this time it is a more powerful and potent one, because the reflections Life is handing to you are too great to ignore. They are 'forcing' you to get involved, to have a more conscious emotional response to what is happening *in* your world, *to* your world. There is no 'them and us', there is only 'us', 'we the people', as humanity. All are brought together by an 'outrage' that affects all. Each person must focus on others besides themself. You must think about and consider others. What you do, or do not do, affects others. All of this is 'forcing' you to be more conscious, more aware of yourself and others.

As a phenomenon, this is highly unusual and extremely remarkable. And even if it is not always conscious in you, it is so powerful that it has changed the energetic makeup of the 'River of Consciousness' around your Earth. Social distancing has created a sense of self-containment, which again can be conscious, subconscious, and unconscious.

This self-containment is not about separation; on a higher level of consciousness, it serves to put you more in touch with yourself and those loved ones you share your life with. This can accentuate your giving and receiving. This can also allow you to be more conscious of how you conduct yourself in your energetic exchanges with others.

As everything has slowed down there is an opportunity to practice patience. Things cannot be rushed. You have to stop rushing here and there and everywhere. All of this adds up to a significant change in the world consciousness. It is a time when spiritual communities everywhere — who are focused on the Light and uplifting consciousness through prayer and meditation — are contributing enormously to the Great Change in The River of Consciousness. The subtleties of Life are now more upfront, more on the surface, so you are more sensitively engaged with everything because subtlety allows that, and creates that as consciousness.

All of this is the creation of a foundation for the continual presence of Super consciousness, as the Christ-Buddha Consciousness, as Ascension, and as Illumination. The creation of this threshold, this platform of foundation, is to give humanity as a whole a more probable opportunity to evolve your consciousness — as soul — to a higher vibration. This is everyone assisting each other to bring about this Great Shift in consciousness.

This is a very positive and powerful energy that is being born now on this planet. And once experienced it will be difficult for humanity to digress from it. This means that upon this new foundation a new and different life can now be seeded, fertilized, and watered here.

As your beginning, this is a time to bypass the economic machine and your personal reliance on being provided *with* and *for*. This world is the one village. And as families of nations and races, you are all within it as lifestyle and living standards, a village in which everyone shares equally. Everyone gives and receives from the village equally.

The village elders come from many different traditions, and each is honored equally. The elders speak with their peoples, and then in council for their peoples. The purpose of the council is to harmonize the village as one voice, one people, one purpose, as the caretaking and promoting of each individual as their dharma and destiny. The village has its mystics as female and male. Those who embody the essence of all that the village aspires to as a collective unity, based within the Universal Principles of Light.

Humanity, this is your moment to seed and impregnate such a vision with life-force gathered from Spirit realms, through prayer, chant, and meditation. Place your vision, as consciousness, within the ethers that we are calling the River of Consciousness.

Whatever may be handed to you by the Dark, know that the Light will always accept it as an opportunity to infuse it with the Light. This is how you can, as personal responsibility, participate *with* the Light, *within* the Light, *as* the Light at this auspicious time for your world and its peoples.

You are surrounded by Light — as the Heavens and the Sky above you — to assist you to transmute what has for so long been the energies of your Earth. The Great Ones have awaited this opportunity to arrive here, when enough people sense and feel Oneness, a Sameness, as a singular focus of healing life everywhere for everyone, and for all living things.

This, as desire, as wish, as dream, as prayer, and as meditation, has given permission for your Sky brothers and sisters to move into a greater and more assistive role as transmutation, and as cleansing and healing.

This is how the Brotherhood of the Light has been able to become more powerfully assistive to the elevation of humanities consciousness. They have also become the paramount Light that is now assisting Mother Earth in her regeneration of new Life after the cataclysmic fires that engulfed Australia in recent times, and the floods, droughts and fires that have affected so many more elsewhere.

Regardless of this destruction of the lands of many nations and the life of these lands, the Grace of Life Itself through the Brotherhood of the Light and the Sisterhood of the Ruby Cross are now reincarnating life back into form and expression of so many of the 'little ones' who lost their lives in the outrage that has been these fires and floods.

Not only has the Dark, as greed and power, not succeeded, but it has granted the Light, waiting in the wings of these outrageous events, an opportunity to come forth in beauteous and magnificent power. Pulling the Light as consciousness through the very center of these Dark events to now be seated equally — and in many instances more powerfully — in front and beside, behind and above and below, so that the Dark Agenda of greed and power is surrounded. And this surrounding will only grow in strength and power, for there is no turning back, no matter how many more times this Dark Agenda attempts to maintain its stranglehold on the lives of humanity and the consciousness of this Earth plane and its life.

What has been, has been. What is, is. What will be, will be. There is a liberation in consciousness that is now afoot, in which humanity in numbers are talking and feeling and thinking about a whole different life for everyone on this Earth. A more brilliant life. Lighter, easier, happier, more creative, more inspiring, more outreaching, not just for those upon this Earth but for Life everywhere.

You have been maintained as life on this Plane as smallness and as an insignificance. You have been kept in this state through a life of survival in which your focus always had to be on yourself and your immediate loved ones.

Such a strength of focus has always been the design of the Dark Agenda. The deflating of your consciousness maintained you in this condition, focused only on sustaining, as best you could, the life of the body. With such a focus, it was deemed that there would be little time or inclination to focus on Spirit. To spend time focused, even in contemplation, on anything beyond human physical survival, was not deemed to have been possible.

If you wanted to concentrate on this, then you would have to remove yourself from this 'survival human' as your focus. And in that, liberate yourself as consciousness whilst in isolation, either in a cave, an ashram, a monastery or any other withdrawal from the world as civilized life expression and form.

All this to create a simple, more pristine environment in which Spirit was central. Centered in a simple focus of "giving your life to God" in a monastery or nunnery, or centered within the presence of a Master, in the East. In the shamanic traditions of indigenous peoples everywhere, there was always, the 'knower', the one with the power who was available to any student who wanted to walk that path.

That is not what is happening now. Yes, there are openings and opportunities for those whose destiny it is to walk such a path. But in these great times the awakening is global. The ashram, the cave, the monastery, the nunnery is global. No matter where you are in your life, living your life, you are in that cave, you are in that ashram, you are in that monastery or nunnery. And it is not about being celibate. It is whatever is your soul's preference, whatever your soul's evolutionary path of awakening is.

It is about the world, as Life everywhere. It is about your family and your fellowship of friends. It is about your soul's lineage, known and unknown by you, no matter who they are and where they are either on this Earth plane or another, either incarnate or discarnate in Spirit realms. All are important. All are significant. All are a part of this Great Awakening.

Whatever is your life path, this too has a great

opportunity to be more aligned to the consciousness of change, as your display of life changes. This is very exciting for every human who wants to move into a more fulfilling expression of their skills and gifts. More aligned to the wisdom gathered through soul journey through lifetimes.

So, awakening can change what you do in the world as your personal unique service to life, which includes service to Mother Earth, service to all Life here and everywhere, and service to your humanity of souls. True service is inclusive of all of them in some way. So, everything you do as true service will have an effect on each of them. This inclusiveness will grant you the deepest fulfilment, the greater sense of Love as gratitude and appreciation for being able to give this great service.

And what you give as service is returned to you one-hundredfold. Returned to you as greater and greater awakening. And with that, higher and more boundless service to Life everywhere. Once you begin a path of service there is no end to it. It is infinite. Journeyed and experienced as Life infinitely on and on forever.

These current times confound many of humankind. They do not understand what it is that *has* happened and *is* happening to their lives and to their world. This is what prayer, chant, meditation, and other healing modalities must be focused upon now. To be of assistance in Spirit—and in life—to those who want understanding; and to give it gently, compassionately, so that they have time to digest and integrate what is being handed to them as the truth of how life has been on this Earth.

To know that their struggles, their confusion, their apathy, their pain and suffering as sadness and grief, as anger and frustration and even rage, is within them because of the overwhelming sense of helplessness and the unfairness that is the constant display of life as 'the way it is' on this Earth plane.

The beauty of Life was stolen from you and replaced with life as a Dark Agenda, as constant war, constant separation as 'them and us', and constant struggle: financially, racially and internationally. Constant indoctrination through media entertainment, politically, economically, and religiously that this is the 'way of life' for you and your peoples of Earth.

But Mother, as Nature, as the Flow of Life, here, and throughout all Existence, is always the movement of harmonizing and balancing. Any life-form that steps into this Flow, with an intent to manipulate and control it, will find themselves having limited success within and on any timeline. And eventually they too will be integrated into the Flow, whether it be through physical death personally or the destruction of their civilization as control, power and greed.

You live now within this time when the Flow of The Mother Goddess, as Pre-Eminence, has entered your world and will bring this Aberration, as life, back into the natural flow of Life, as was always intended *from* and *within* the One Beginning.

This means that all who are aligned to this Aberration must find somewhere else, some other timeline in some other Universe that will allow their chaos to live and exist. It is no longer for this world. It is the time now for you as consciousness, as all living expressions, to consider Liberation and Freedom.

What will you do with it?

Each soul must awaken to the dream they hold—that they passionately desire—to manifest within the consciousness of harmony and balance. *You have one.*

Every soul, at this time, holds to a dream for a greater life expression and experience for themselves, and all, and everyone. This is your time to let it dawn upon your hearts and minds. Pray for this to occur. Chant, pray, and meditate for this to birth in you and become you and your life.

These are magnificent times, extraordinary times, in which everything and anything is possible. Birth in Love your excitement, your joy, your happiness, your compassion, and your peace for what is possible as your contribution, as your life in service.

I love you.

So be it.

Harmony or Disharmony

My Beloved One,

The single most important feature of your life, at this time, is to have a constant conscious recognition that these are new times — within a new consciousness — that have never been simpler or easier for you to tap into as your daily life in the world you live in.

You have never been more interconnected, as a world consciousness, to these higher levels of consciousness that in dimensional understanding you may call higher fourth and fifth. However, given that you and your Earth plane are primarily existing in third-dimensional consciousness you will still largely be feeling the effects of this influence.

But if you ask yourself the question, "How conscious do I want to become?" You will realize, as your answer, that you will want to experience a greater self-awareness than what the old consciousness gave you as life. For this to occur it will be necessary for you to take charge, as self-responsibility, for seeking a greater alignment to yourself as consciousness. All that you are looking to move into as Existence, as Life, already exists, so it is that you will simply arrive, as your remembering, at this new state of awareness.

THE WRITINGS

There are many different centres of Light upon your world offering you initiations, in which a framework is given that becomes the focus of your attention—your fixity—as you move into these higher states of consciousness. It becomes a home, a state, in which you can begin to build a level of familiarity in which you may speak, "This is the new consciousness that I reside within."

Each soul has an attunement at this time, and this will be felt as an interest, a desire, a curiosity, and a willingness to move towards a particular centre of Light. Whether, or not, you fully realise you are moving to a place, a state, within your hologram of Self that will best feed you your own desire for further awakening is not important. Whether it is here on this incarnate world, or the Spirit realms of Heaven upon the 'other side', you will continue to move into higher states within the hologram of the Self.

There are always those whose Divine purpose is to work with you, within both the incarnate worlds and the Spirit worlds. Their work, as purpose, is to constantly be an existence within whatever state you are currently fixed upon within your hologram of the Self. Everything you experience within this state, at whatever level, is aiming to assist you to fulfil your understandings, as a 'known', and then to move you into the next level of more expanded knowing, as your new state of self-awareness within the infinitely expanding hologram of the One Self.

Harmony or Disharmony

Sometimes as a student of Life, as a seeker upon a path, you will feel you have reached your 'highest truth' as your knowing of your Divinity. This is not possible, particularly from within your human incarnate state of existence. All you must know and appreciate is that you are upon a path of infinite expansion, and where your soul alignment is pointing you is where you need to go next, as a gateway, doorway, or portal of expanding consciousness.

Do not try to figure it all out within the human perceptions of your spiritual path and spiritual direction; simply be aware that change, as expansion, will be moved towards as part of your hologram of Self. Your human role, more than anything else, is to be aware of your own movement, as thought, as emotion, as your life path. This movement can block change, slow the movement of change, or assist change. Be aware and be truthful with yourself concerning the influence of your ego human mind and emotional self. You say there is plenty of time to do this. Time for what? Time for who? If you look at it with an open mind, this is simply the voice of procrastination.

What do you gain from such an exercise? To remain centred as consciousness within the old human ego self may grant you the tried-and-true familiarity you are comfortable with, but it will not give you any relief from the 'vegetative state' you are 'asleep' within, in which you are not truly alive to the Self. To not be alive to the Self holds you in a state of limbo. A state that holds you separated from everyone and everything. You may not feel entirely separated, but you are because you are not connecting with the One Self you are within all. To not connect at this level of consciousness is to breathe the shallow breath of, "I am this body."

If this is your only breath then you are committing yourself to only experience life as the ups-and-downs of the body, the youthfulness or ageing of the body, the birthing, living, and dying of the body. Such a limited expression and experience can only hand you a very small measure of happiness and joy, and holds you open to an inordinate amount of physical, mental, and emotional pain and suffering. The body breath, as body consciousness, cannot give to you the fulfilment you truly, deeply desire. Body consciousness is not love for most. Love must be breathed into the body, must be given to the body and the body must be open to receive it. As consciousness, you must elevate above the complacency that is the hallmark of the body ego consciousness.

To *elevate* means that you must step outside and beyond such a limiting awareness as yourself and your life. To do this you must act, and that can only occur as the active presence of a deeper, stronger desire that is penetrating the 'old' human body consciousness. This desire is from within the Heart of Love that you truly are. Such a state of existence does

Harmony or Disharmony

not hold doubt or uncertainty, as ignorance, about the truth of your nature, that is beyond the influence of time and any of its creations. It is the immeasurable and everlasting Self you are.

The human nature is a creation *of* Time; therefore, it is continuously influenced *by* Time. To be continuously influenced by Time means that it must bow to the 'reality' of change. Change is everywhere and change is within everything. Within change, the state of perfection can only exist as Allowance in which you hold yourself present in the knowing that all *must be* allowed, all *is* allowed. Allowed means the complete absence of judgement. The complete absence of all and any opinion. As human nature you rigidly hold to this, as your mechanism of definition, in which you define yourself, life, and your reality within it.

Your torment and suffering exist as *you* because, as body consciousness, the self is recognised and known only by its judgements and its opinions. This is the inner 'rat race' called life on Earth. This you content yourself with—watching and participating in—as your external human life, which is only a reflection. It only exists this way because you constantly harbour and nurture this as life within you. If you want more, if you want something different, then you must seek to know yourself as True Nature: the unchangeable nature of Self that you are.

To *know* means you must take action to readjust your mental and emotional focus. Take time to readjust your physical focus. This is the path. And now, at this time, the path is open, open to everyone everywhere. Your choices every day are to have your life reflect your own willingness to make movement upon the path as your own awakening. The path is the same everywhere, for everyone, as the movement in consciousness back into the unchangeable Self you are, as your primary awareness.

Where you connect and how you connect is a reflection of your soul. The soul is always in a state of readiness at a particular level of evolutionary status, and this cannot be fully appreciated by you within your human mind which is a 'new creation' in each lifetime. It does not have the breadth of vision, the perspective, that allows this to be known and understood. So, any talk of understanding the nature of the soul must come from a higher source of Wisdom. This Wisdom, for some, may be included in the state of your present level of awareness, so there will be some understanding of the soul's nature.

But the floodgates of awareness will not open until you return to the soul as 'I am'. To do this you must relinquish your dependency on wanting to understand yourself and your life through the inauspiciousness of your 'only human' mind and intellect. The soul is a panoramic state of consciousness so vast that within your human state you would fall to the ground and call it God. In worshipping the soul, you are indeed bowing to its

Harmony or Disharmony

Creator that is *within it* as Divinity, and *beyond it* as Divinity.

Beyond is the already existing state of the Divine Self you are, that as soul, you have not recognised and therefore cannot hold as 'I am'. The soul holds you as Divinity and holds you as human. It is the lifeboat you created as Divine Consciousness to constantly be there for you as human, to hold you and sustain you through all your journeys.

Is the soul everlasting? You can only know this from within the state of the soul in which your own evolving remembrance of your Divinity — within the Dual Nature of the Divine — will offer to you, will hold open to you, the inevitability of that possibility. Until that moment arrives as your awakening, you may want to deify the soul you are as your most immediate and tangible thread of Light that can pull you into your Divine Nature. At its highest state, the soul holds for you the essences of consciousness you are as Divine Nature. These essences are given to the human aspect of the soul from within the Christ-Buddha consciousness. This level of consciousness holds open the human aspect of the soul and holds it as a creation.

Your soul is the doorway into your Enlightened state of existence. 'Awakening' is really the steps you take as movement in consciousness into the soul state. Awakening involves you in greater knowing: greater knowing of the human nature self, and greater knowing of the True Nature Divine Self. Because the soul is both of these natures, you cannot choose to accept one and deny the other. You cannot praise one and denigrate the other. You cannot place more importance on one over the other. You must simply acknowledge the necessity to surrender into the state of non-judgement in which the order of all things acknowledges that to exist — as Presence in God — is to be present in both. Present in both, in the state of non-judgement, gives you your human life, ruled by your soul's destiny and your soul's purpose.

In this, the Christ-Buddha consciousness truly becomes present as your peace, as your continuous loving acceptance, as your acknowledged power, as your created life, as journey, as experience, and as expression. This is alignment: alignment to Self, alignment to Life, alignment to the Christ-Buddha consciousness you are. And as this, your alignment to the soul becomes truly profound and divinely meaningful. For each of you this alignment will be the steps you take as an awakening one. And the more often you revisit this as contemplation, as Wisdom, as meditation, and as 'life practice', the more you will begin to harmonize the two natures within the soul, and in that the two natures within the Self as the One Beginning you are.

Is this Wisdom necessary at this time? Let your soul answer that. Let your soul *be the answer* to that. Give yourself the time and the space, as opportunity, to see how you — as soul — respond. Not you as human ego,

Harmony or Disharmony

but you as the two-fold nature of the One you are, that is held as soul self-understanding. Recognition will not come to you simply through wanting it.

You must work at it. You must make effort. You must commit minutes in each day to focus upon, "I want to change. I feel change within me, calling out to my conscious heart and mind. Let's do this, read this, go there, meet these people, go on this adventure."

It is 'newness', it is 'different' calling to you as it must. And the call is from within the soul reaching into your current preoccupations as life, suggesting to you the need to harmonise. To harmonise within your soul, to harmonise with your Self, and to harmonise with Life everywhere.

Each soul has within it the history of journey, and so it knows exactly the state of your current journey, as your life, and it is holding the knowing of all the 'issues' you are being called to harmonise with. Issues are the antithesis of harmony. Issues are what you are currently disharmonising with. Issues are what you are currently unable to 'awaken' within. You are preferring the 'sleep' of judgement in which you believe your opinions really matter and that your perceptions are a 'truth' of any consequence.

Whatever holds your attention must be looked at in terms of harmony. All harmony is your natural inner state of being. Disharmony says, "I will not go there, I cannot go there, I refuse to go there." Wherever 'there' happens to be as a harmonising consciousness. Such 'self-importance' affects nobody, but yourself. It becomes the held onto battlefield you will not walk away from, so convinced are you that the enemy is indeed real.

The enemy only exists in the state of consciousness in which you express and experience a continuous willingness, as refusal, not to harmonise with the highest nature of your soul, as the Self. All ridicule is only your own ridiculing of yourself for not choosing harmony, for not choosing peace, and in that, for not choosing to acknowledge the great importance of you as soul.

Jesus did not come to save your souls. He came to give you the opportunity to evolve your own soul. Jesus forgiving you is meaningless if you do not forgive yourself and all others. True forgiveness can only occur as you begin to harmonize your existence, as your life, both inwardly and outwardly.

Harmony is only possible as a continuous moment-to-moment state of letting go. Letting this go and that go, letting him go and her go, and letting them go. Letting go moment-to-moment is you living in the unimportance of all projections placed upon you and those you place upon others.

Unimportance and detachment do not mean you do not care, but that your caring is taking place within a higher consciousness in which compassion resides, and happiness and joy live. The higher state of gratitude and appreciation, as Love, is wanting only the very best for yourself and all others. This is your moment-to-moment awareness that harmony works for you as your day-to-day life.

And all this, as self-expression and experience, must be consciously practised and experienced. It must be fed, and it is you who must feed it. And the food you feed it comes to you from your soul as life direction, as life purpose, as personal soul destiny.

You must awaken more and move into the state of Trust. This is only possible as an indication of your willingness to trust your soul's input into your life.

The more you call for and acknowledge this input when it occurs, the more that acknowledgement — as happiness and joy, as compassion and peace, as gratitude and appreciation, as love of Life and love of your life, as fulfilment — becomes the consciousness you are choosing as your 'I am', as self-awareness.

This brings to you the experience of the subtle power that is Love. A power that does not override, but permeates and penetrates and causes healing of every conceivable kind to occur within yourself and all life everywhere. This is the new state of the mind and the heart that is beginning to truly come alive on this beautiful Earth and everywhere.

You are here to cause this change to become greater and more magnificent, moment-to-moment as your personal self, as your personal life, and as your personal world.

THE WRITINGS

Trust this movement within you. It is wanting to blossom within you and all around you now.

I love you.

So be it.

You, as Precious Life

My Beloved One,

Fruitful times in your life can occur once you have successfully traversed a Great Crossing that has placed you upon another Shore, another Land. It is the Sea of Consciousness you have been sailing upon, and the Great Spirit of The One has been the Boat you have been seated within. The Sails that caught the Winds of Liberation, too, were this Great Spirit of Love.

You can never know with any surety when you will find yourself upon this Ocean of Consciousness, living within heightened Life that is calling you to Awaken into greater actions of Love. Knowing that Precious Existence is Life everywhere, life to you in your world, precious life of those around you in all their different varieties of form and expression, and those that you experience as utmost importance. The ones you do not want to be separated from, taken from you — or for you to be taken from them. They are 'life change' for you.

And within this 'life change', upon the Ocean of Consciousness, there is always the Great Spirit of The One, the Divine Holy Spirit of Love holding you, holding this one and that one, holding Life and allowing Change. Allowing circumstances to rise as the ocean tides causing you to run towards or run away. Causing you to fall into the numbness of 'sleep', unaware that the rising tide of Consciousness is *with* you now, *within* you now, calling to your soul, your soul calling you,

"Please respond. Please make movement into greater Life, more Life, and the realization of Life as precious."

Yes, you are precious. All those you love are precious, and Life all around you is precious. You cannot truly move into this conscious-aware state of appreciation until you walk up to that edge, that brink of extinction, in which what you have, what you love, what you cherish, what loves you, cherishes you and adores you, can be taken from you as real or considered.

This is the movement of Life in your perceptual world in which birth, life, and death are real, true, and unmistakably tangible to your body senses, the body mind and emotions, and the body world of life on this Earth. The fragile nature of your perceptions. The fragile nature of your life and death 'reality'. The fragile nature of love, of peace, of harmony, compassion and forgiveness, tolerance and allowance. It is so easy to hold them up as highest focus until life and death, as perception, fully arises *before* you or *within* you. The specter of David and Goliath arises within you as real choice.

You know you must choose. All that has hidden life and death choice from you has been stripped from you. The constant presence of the—placated and

You, as Precious Life

placating—human mind emotions has thus been instantaneously cast aside. The false luxury, the false reality, and the false truth stripped from you. Your soul is laid bare. You are now living in the immediacy of your life. The soul self is present. The cloned and constantly cloning human nature is, in such moments, such times, nullified, neutralized, vaporized; and the real you, the upholder of Life in the face of death, the you that knows beyond doubt, beyond reason, beyond all explanation that Life, precious Life, must be allowed. Life to *have*, Life to *be*, Life to *live*.

This is the Spirit of Life you are possessed by, and you will take hold, embrace, and make yours as Self as 'I' and as 'Am'. This as Identity, this as who you are, is the awesome experience, the awesome presence, as great as you can be, as declaration, as emphatic Truth.

*"I am Life. I choose Life. Life it must be.
Life it is, only Life."*

Life for you and the precious life you call your loved ones, those that are your family of love, the ones you live with and experience life with. They, who are important to you, are transfixed by the intensity of your focus when you speak, "There is only Life."

This is the Presence of God by any name. This is the Presence, by whatever name, as your level of understanding or confusion. The Presence of The One as the Presence of Life holds you and your whole existence including those most loved, most cherished by you, and the Presence speaks to you through all of your life circumstances.

"Choose Life. Do you choose Life?"

And if the answer is, "Yes", then you are changed forever in that moment. Your soul has undergone further awakening in such times and experiences. Awakening that moves you to another level of life appreciation and the knowing that the value, the worth, and the significance of all Life will grow within you. And those loved ones, most precious, near and dear to you, will be gazed upon by you, more intimately, more filled with wonder than ever before, for their life is magnificent and blessed. The heart connection will be acknowledged on a deeper level than before and this heart connection is a direct channel to their soul. And in love, as heartfelt feelings, you carry that hidden Song of Life back into their soul. From their soul to your soul, your soul to their soul, as the Truth of the Circle of Life, the Circle of Love.

The scourge of not knowing, of not caring or realizing, is removed from you in those moments, and as your awakening, has the potential to never return you to complete unawareness again. Your soul has experienced the excitation of 'Awakening' which is communion and connection, is the experience of being known, and of knowing.

You are precious Life beyond the body consciousness. You awaken as realization, as awareness of Life within a center of Consciousness that you may have been 'asleep' to for most of this lifetime. Once you feel that

You, as Precious Life

palpable energy of soul life, the soul existence you are, then you cannot completely return to numbness and 'sleep'. Unless through actions taken, you defy the knowing and the practices of generating gratitude and appreciation for the preciousness of all Life everywhere.

This is, as awakening, your realization that Love is the very core of Life. The very core of your experience of relationship. Love that is beyond words, beyond the moment-to-moment exchanges you call 'living your human life'. This is the deeper energy, the engine room that is the power that moves all Life, all actions, all having a life, in any form as relationship exchange. Love pulls you in deeper and deeper. Love, as eternal Life, knows no limits as to where your realizations and your appreciation can reside within.

The exquisite beauty, as the core of your Divine Soul, is where the food of Love is held for you to have and to taste, in this experience and in that experience. And the shock and surprises in your life that cause you to exclaim, "I never saw this coming," is the hallmark of those moments of opportunity in which true awakening, as greater awareness and appreciation for your life and all Life, occurs. There are further experiences awaiting you. You will never know when those moments are until you are within the life of that experience.

The karmas that unite two souls, three souls or any number of souls, as 'locked in' to one particular experience, one life changing experience, sometimes cannot be fully appreciated until after the event has occurred. Or perhaps during the most heightened awareness, as the crescendo, as the brink, as the edge, or as the wave is about to break and come crashing down.

Those 'out of body' experiences and moments are when you, in an 'altered state', are subliminally connected to your soul, and through that, the souls of all others involved in the experience. You 'forget' all other aspects of your human self. They are forgotten and let go of as influence, as worthy of consideration. They melt into that space of 'letting go' where 'importance' as perception rules everything.

Instead, you are carried by the Stream of Life, as the Stream of Consciousness, into the soul's realms of the Undeniable, in which there is certainly no room for 'consideration', there is only the driving force of Life, of the one precious Life everywhere that opens your heart, and opens your mind to the everlasting fruitfulness of greater Life, in which your actions are actions of, "I must." Your emotions, as passion, are the absolute knowing, "I must."

And the mind—aligned in those moments to the Father Holy Spirit of The One—knows only to speak of Life, to acknowledge precious Life, and to do what must be done to bring about the continuation of precious Life everywhere. The experience is liberating for the consciousness and, therefore, liberating for

You, as Precious Life

your human life. You will feel lighter, clearer, and cleaner; more 'in love' with everyone and everything, including your own self as precious Life.

There is a connection that you Awaken into that can be nourished every day in every way. The connection is to Life, you to Life. In this, Life takes on a new importance and a new significance. You realize more clearly that you can feed Life, and in that you feel fed by Life. Not necessarily those you feed as life, but by Life itself. Life the Immeasurable. Life the Unknown. Life that is Love, Life that is Service in which what is given out returns to you as Life.

Life feeds Life.

It is never about the responses and reactions of those you feed. It is not about whether they value or appreciate, or can even feel, how you are feeding them. Life knows. Life feels. Life gives back. This is all going on inside you as the consciousness of the One Life, the consciousness of the one Circle of Life and the consciousness of the One as Service of giving and receiving. You are the giver, and you are the receiver, you as that level of consciousness, are the Circle of Life as self-awareness. Once this births within you, Life takes on a different meaning, a different importance, and a completely different 'come from' as Self Presence than what the human ego may call self-presentation.

Self-presentation you have called it, because that is what you know, understand, and admit to as human ego self. But Self Presence is a more pure and more refined experience. It is the preciousness of all Life importance, not the ego self-preservation importance that you have created to live within and 'survive' within.

This begins the awareness of the path as service to the preciousness of all Life. In an Eastern spiritual context, it has been known for thousands of years as the path of the Bodhisattva. The one whose life is committed to the preservation and the uplifting of precious Life everywhere. This is life *in* Service, *as* Service, in which each moment of focus in such a state of awareness is a moment to walk the path of Enlightenment in which Life is central, Service is core, and Love imbues all actions with compassion and caring.

The purity of this path is undeniable. No matter what karmas the personal life may still be involved within — or may have been involved within, or is yet to be involved within — the strength and the courage to override all challenges, all difficulties, and remain ever-present in this higher consciousness of service to Life, service to Love, and service to the One Spirit of All, will always override, will always meld with the karmas yet to be resolved as 'released from'. It will speed up this release, and as service to Life dissolve the 'hold' that these karmas may still have on you.

This is devotion, this is *Bakti*: love of the Way, love of the Path. The Way is no longer viewed as a path of self-discipline or self-control. It is no longer the sliding scale of 'struggle' in which you are constantly doing battle with what you view as right or higher or more refined. In which you are constantly in doubt as, "Can I get there, be it, in this situation, in this circumstance?"

You have glided, sailed if you will, beyond that. And now you find yourself seated as 'this is who I am' within a higher state that is you birthing self-containment, in which you are no longer needy, you are no longer starving to be fed by your personal addictions. You feel a balance and a harmony in which you are seated as conscious awareness. So, you can give that harmony, you can give that wisdom of balance to others. You, the teacher, you the friend, you the lover or loved one, you the bodhisattva. You have found a level of the Self that you know is Truth, is Life, beyond the contamination of the 'lost' human mind and human heart, buried as they are within the question, the doubt, the confusion of, "who am I?"

The power you have become is truly subtle because it is carried as 'Innocence' within Love. As Shakti, It cannot be truly seen for the awesomeness it is. Love coats it with peace, with beauty, with charm, with elegance, with whatever will feed the human ego's need to feel,

"I am in the presence of something greater, something that is from the Beyond, and as that is imbued with the Spirit of, a taste of, a fragrance of Life that I do not know, I do not understand and, therefore, I do not yet appreciate."

THE WRITINGS

But you know you would want that. You know you must have that. You must know yourself as Shakti. You must know yourself as power within Love, joined and merged as that awesome benevolence in which the preciousness of all Life is known, is felt and, therefore, is irrefutably upheld. This is the Consciousness of The One. You cannot go beyond this for The One is everything. You can only know more deeply. You can only feel more deeply. You, in such profoundness, must become more and more Self-contained.

You desire it, want it, you must have it. Your whole being is becoming filled with the merging. the merging beyond choice. The merging within "I Am". This is the Home that is truly you.

I welcome you Home. I want you Home now.

I love you.

So be it.

The Essence of 'I am only human'

My Beloved One,

Each time you take a step, as a conscious choice, towards your Awakened state you are strengthening the core of who you truly are. You are Love. You are Peace. You are happiness and joy. You are the celebration of Life in all its forms and varieties, in all its expressions and experiences as they come upon you and you upon them.

In this approach to your life, and to Life everywhere, you have let go of the need to 'navigate'. Such a need resides within the human ego nature as the emotional state of fear, and lack of trust. To navigate is necessary so that you move through your life in a way that 'protects' you. But this perception of 'protection' is borne out of pain and held within pain. Protection then is to guard you from further pain. Pain and suffering within any human keeps you in disbelief about your own magnificence, even when you speak words to the contrary.

Pain and suffering is the essence of 'I am only human' as your nature. 'I am only human' arose within you as a statement, as an announcement to yourself and your world once you had succumbed to, "I am my pain and suffering." No human, who as consciousness resides only within their human nature state, is free of pain and suffering. Your life, your personality, your beliefs, your dreams have all been created through pain and suffering. What you want to have and hold on to, what you want to be free of and escape from, is always about you wanting not to be in pain and suffering. As your life, you will surround yourself with the play of distraction: hoping, wishing, wanting, dreaming, forcing, demanding, conniving and manipulating it to be different. Wanting it not to be the obviousness of pain and suffering.

And if that is not possible — which it is not — then you must enter the multiplicity and abundant expressions and experiences of denial. Denial, that is pain and suffering in the body. Denial, that is the constant confusion and worry in your state of mind. Denial, that is the constant seeking of anything to cover over the unhappiness and lack of fulfilment in your life.

Instead, you have momentary experiences of 'feel good' within your life of addictions. Life created from within your human nature can only ever be a life of addiction because addiction is your human nature's means of attempting to experience happiness and joy. The times in which you say you are in happiness and joy are easily distracted by other parts of you, as personality life, that are not happy, and that have needs that must be paid attention to. And all of this is mainly hidden in the fog of confusion you call being

The Essence of 'I am only human'

human and having a 'normal' human life.

'Normal' is pain and suffering as consciousness. Normal is denial as your multiple addictions. Your addictions, as consciousness, are the state of never being satisfied. Never being satisfied, as a seesaw, can tilt your life either way. On the one hand, you can succumb to a life of mediocrity in which your enthusiasm for life falls away. On the other hand, you can fill your life with ambition, and in that substitute enthusiasm for life with enthusiasm for 'how great am I', as human nature expression.

The lack of continuity that is the result of living unawakened as consciousness, means you will always be jumping from one thing to another: one need, one addiction, one belief, one judgement, one pain, one suffering. So, the human nature consciousness will never fulfil you, no matter how much your world fills you with its 'entertainment.'

The human nature consciousness is a distracted nature, so your consumer one-world-village was created from within this nature, by this nature, to appease this nature. So, there is no point judging it for it is your creation, it is your need, your desire, and your state of consciousness as confusion. Your world, your economic machine is a creation of humanity's pain and suffering, and in that humanity's denial consciousness.

Greed, of any description, cannot be judged as a standalone fault in any human. It is a consequence of a deeper malaise. Attempting to change greed as a character flaw without addressing the consciousness of the human nature is not useful as either contemplation or discussion. It is not the core issue. It is not the root of all inequality. Selfishness, as the overwhelming 'worry', lives permanently in pain and suffering consciousness. Worry, as not trusting, means "I have to look after me first."

Having to 'look after me first' never truly changes even in relationships, even in family, because family at the level of human nature is still the merry-go-round, the whirlpool of pain and suffering. And if and when necessary, conscious denial and subconscious denial allow feelings to be suppressed and subjugated in order to be 'responsible.' Relationships and families have responsibilities, and that is the glue that holds them together. Responsibility can be a standalone sense as a recognition, and in that, personal feelings and needs are set aside. Or responsibility may be infused with love, with grace, blessings, and appreciation. So, it is a willingness, as commitment, to take on the experience. But you know through personal experience that this does not override all of your life as experience. It does not take from you the pain and suffering consciousness that is more obvious in other parts of your life.

It is difficult for any human to truly address this with any degree of comfort because the human ego will quickly jump in and defend and justify. Especially if

The Essence of 'I am only human'

you only have the human nature consciousness as your appreciation of who you are. In this unawakened state there is no alternative, there is nowhere else as consciousness for you to go. You are stuck within its limitations.

What will you do about it? Is there anything that you can do? Are you interested at all in moving outside these boundaries? Do you want something more than pain and suffering consciousness?

These questions require consideration because they involve commitment. Commitment to a change in course, a change in direction, a change in awareness, a change in focus, as change in consciousness. This is a significant alteration to who you have become so accustomed to being. It is a different energy, and it can only become you by a commitment to consistently embrace it. This can only be done through consistent practices that are outside your acquired habits built within the consciousness of pain and suffering.

All that is 'usual'—as your emotional habits, your mind habits, and your physical habits—are all habits of pain and suffering, that are your habits of addiction, your habits of selfishness, and your habits of denial. The comprehensiveness of this consciousness is so pervasive within you and everyone around you as your culture and societies, and as your nations, that significant 'other world' connections must be allowed to enter you and your life. And they will do so once you energize your commitment to undertake change.

THE WRITINGS

There really is no point diagnosing your pain and suffering. The *'where* it is', the *'how* it is,' the *'when* it is,' and the *'why* it is' can be identified as unique to you and as an acknowledgement of, "Yes I am the product, as human nature, of all my pain and suffering."

Once acknowledged, you must move beyond the temptation, either by you or your therapist, to fix it. It cannot be fixed. The consciousness of pain and suffering cannot be fixed. It is what it is. It must be moved beyond. You must, as choice, set it aside and begin to build another awareness of self: another awareness emotionally, mentally, physically, and spiritually. You are wanting to embrace the consciousness of a different identity with a different nature which we will call your True Nature.

True Nature speaks of another beginning, beyond you as human in this lifetime. True Nature, as beginning, is Divine in essence and origin. True Nature, if chosen by you, is your beginning in this lifetime upon a spiritual path. The spiritual path of Truth will give you another understanding of yourself. It will give you the understanding of a more profound origin than the physical birthing of you as a human body. It will take you beyond the stars and universes. It will take you beyond all appreciation of any and all dimensions of Life. It will re-inform you of your one true Beginning and you to your Self within and as that Beginning One.

For many who have begun such a journey you must know that the consciousness of pain and suffering is

The Essence of 'I am only human'

very sticky. It feels good and right to blame and judge and feel justification. It feels comforting to indulge addictive habits and behaviors. It creates the sticky state of, "I am satisfied with this."

To be satisfied is the defensiveness of collapsing back into the state of no effort, no real change. It is the state of the familiar, in which you can have all of your reasons and understandings. You can have the comfort of the fabricated state of 'autonomy' in which you believe you are truly deciding anything of any importance, when in fact you are simply slip-sliding from one cover-up to the next. One feelgood moment of, "I am satisfied" to the next, and one unconscious moment of 'sleep' to the next.

To not want to awaken, or to believe, in your autonomous human ego state, that you can orchestrate your own awakening in your own timing in the way that suits you — as not being or feeling challenged — is an illusion. It is you creating another mask that you will, at some point, have to release yourself from. You will have to unmask, come out of hiding and call it what it truly is as preference. You prefer the masks you have placed over all of your pain and suffering, and you are calling these masks, that you have spent a lifetime building and maintaining, your 'best work', and in that you are satisfied.

Wisdom from within your masks is always being judged. It is not allowed. It has to undergo all your interpretations of it. So, Wisdom is not fluid and flowing within you and you within Wisdom. You are held back from merging with the Wisdom and that must be acknowledged as your true intention. You do not want to merge. You, in your consciousness of pain and suffering, only want wisdom as another acquired habit that satisfies your need for 'feel good.'

You have entered this world at a very important time. No matter how many lifetimes you have 'sat' in the presence of Wisdom, or if this is your very first, you will have amazing opportunities given to you, at this time, to move beyond the consciousness of pain and suffering. It is always going to be your choice. What do you want as opportunity? What do you want as the next step in your awakening? Which actions are you willing to take that will form new habits that feed your spiritual awakening?

Your life, all of it, can be an expression and experience of your spiritual path. Who you are in the world can be a spiritual path. All of your life can be influenced by higher Wisdom. Influenced in such a way that you will release old patterns of thought and emotion. You will want to set your whole life straight. You will want, not only yourself changed, but your finances, your health, your relationships, your nation and your world. This is truly exciting. For now, at this time, the word 'spiritual' and the word 'path' are reaching into every aspect of your human life as it was always intended.

The power of this time is so significant that it can be

The Essence of 'I am only human'

viewed as possibly being life-altering for everyone everywhere. Such magnitude, such breadth of impact, has never occurred before in this dimension of Life. And what happens here on this Earth plane will affect Life everywhere.

Pain and suffering is so insignificant as consciousness within the big picture of Change that it cannot even be registered within purer realms of Consciousness. That insignificance can highlight for you the lop-sidedness of any decision to remain in that condition, as significance, when you have the whole of God as your possible playground in Consciousness. To look at your own stubborn determination to remain there must be looked at as your own attention to life, that you want life to acknowledge to you how much it has hurt you. The cry within this blame, is, "I am not responsible, I am not willing to *be* responsible or accept that I *am* responsible."

This refusal allows a darkness to live within you as human life, and within you as soul. It will lead you down destructive pathways that are not even recognized or seen as irresponsibility. It is the sickened heart and mind that only wants to submerge itself in life as pain. That can only be seen as the constant seeking of gratification through 'feel good' habits. This is a torturous path for a human to walk, leading as it does into lifetimes of unrequited love. Lost to love, it becomes not believed to exist at all.

The search, the seeking, the longing for love is

epidemic in your societies now, so great has become your 'walk' in the other direction. At this time of Great Change, you are gifting yourself a Renewal. The most significant Renewal your soul has ever experienced. The purpose of these Writings is to help you appreciate the nature, the implications, the path and the results, as this Renewal.

You must know clearly what you are walking into and what you may choose to walk away from. You are owed this. You are that great, that magnificent, that significant. You came to hear this Wisdom in this lifetime. You came to go as far as you possibly can upon your path of Renewal into the vast playground of Divine Consciousness.

The Return is the Renewal in which you are taking the opportunity, blessed upon your soul, to re-awaken into the knowing of yourself as Divinity, as God, as the One. In that re-awakening, pain and suffering as human ego consciousness, will be departed from, left behind as life for you. Held simply in your compassionate heart, accepted for all its limitations.

Refreshed with Divine essence, your life-force is motivating you to move your awareness into the state of,

"I am Love. I am Peace. I am health. I am prosperity. I am spiritually awakening. And all that is granted to me is being granted to everyone everywhere."

The Essence of 'I am only human'

This is you, as higher consciousness. This is you as expanded awareness. This is you living in the True Nature Self, that which is your true home as Self, human and Divine. It has always been that. It will always be that. Become comfortable in the knowing of, and the acceptance of, this Truth.

Then you can truly fly as Consciousness. In this state you are truly Liberated.

I love you.

So be it.

You are your Christ's Dream

My Beloved One,

To be great is to be small. Not in significance and your impact on your world, but in relation to your very existence. You must not seek to be known in a way that is worldly, for that significance bears the attention of a world that seeks to know a celebrity, and that is not your purpose or design. For you have come at a time when all that is before you, as your world, seeks to be known as that which has its own life and its own power. It wants to know its own significance. It wants to tread lightly upon all that lies before it. It wants to be as a carpet of blossoming flower petals strewn upon a walkway that is your blessed life.

You cannot but be impressed with what is Life, for it holds in it a magic of created energy, that allows all of humanity to play, as if you were a child, an innocent one who has no decisions to make, and all is but the fluid moment of wonder that leads you on and on. You are both the spectator and the one who is the creator. And you feel the two inside you, and you wonder which one you truly are. You are both. As you move forward, it is your destiny to unfold the magnificence of your own brilliant Duality.

THE WRITINGS

How can it be that you walk here as one who creates, and you hardly understand that power at all? It does not feel like it belongs to you, but it does. It simply resides, as power, within a state of consciousness you do not have full possession of. But you can and you will. You are your own captivated audience, your own Father-Mother's child, the spellbound relationship of the magician and its audience. You are both. And now is a brilliant time to become more and more aware of the Duality of Consciousness that resides within you as Life. You may speak. "I am that which is the Within, and I am that which is the Without, of all Life."

The Power you possess to create your own existence comes from the Within that is itself multi-layered and multi-faceted. It is not easy for any human to know or understand, but you innately have the ability to utilize the Within. There is such a stigma attached to 'creating life' for some of Humanity for it runs contrary to your own feelings of wanting to be led, and your resignation to being at the mercy of forces beyond you.

The karmas of any lifetime are the perceptions that there is right and wrong, to be and to know. And for you there is always the temptation, the opportunity, to surrender to the inclination of these perceptions. Then you become them—as a label—and so you begin to manufacture the identity that goes with the label. And soon you act upon, and act out, the label and this allows you to become a created fantasy of 'who you are'. Your conditioning—that is the list of possibilities

You are your Christ's Dream

you have been given in order to create the label — gives you your identity, and gives you a truth you can say is real, and then you may act upon it as substantiated. This increases the power of this label as you substantiate it in actions, in thoughts, and in feelings.

You want to know about that Power that lies beneath the surface of all thought and all emotion, that brings to you what you want and that which you say you do not want. There exists within each and every human a Power that is Creator, that speaks not in words, but can utilize them as the springboard to all Life. In the Beginning that has no end, there exists the Juice and the Fire; that is the 'turn on' that never goes away, that is this Creator Power. It is the lust, the passion, that is never satisfied. It is the extraordinary state of Life-charge that lives within you, never satisfied, but always wanting to be and never wanting to be. It is, as the never-released sweetness of pre-orgasm that sits within you, held captive by that which you are as the Creator.

You may have tasted the knowing of this Energy and the knowing of this feeling. You may want it again and again. And that you think it is sexual is true in a sense, but it moves as this Energy outside the realms of the physical loins of the human body. It moves as the Creator force throughout the wholeness of God. It lives within Consciousness as the delight that speaks, "I love Life. I am the Creator who created it."

And it is the sweet ongoing energy of a Power that is

never satisfied and is never not replenished. It is not the disappearing glow of the post-orgasmic state of the human sexual experience. It does not require a body in order to channel the experience of this Energy. You do. And you do not.

A Christed One or a Buddha, is one who wants what it wants, and exists as one who seeks to move beyond all that it is in any given moment as Existence, and as Consciousness. You, as this One, already understand that you are conscious at a level of knowing who you are, as that level of Life. It is a blessed existence that allows you to know that you are a Beginning, and you seek in that Beginning to expand it into a Forever that has the understanding,

"I am the One that is."

And in that, there is the Father, and in that there is the Mother. And the Christ is the man, is the woman, who holds their Forever whilst they walk upon a world that has no understanding of Forever. For Life here on your world is a Dream created, and it is a fullness that is an emptiness. And it is fabricated so that Life and Love can be explored over and over through Time. You are not that which is labeled this or that, for that is only a creation to explore the one you are in journey, in which you speak.

"If I am this, in this exploration, what is it that I feel? What is it that I know? What is it I understand now about myself and Life?"

You are your Christ's Dream

The Juice of any experience is to speak, "I know who I am." For you it is felt in human terms and human understandings. There is comfort or discomfort in that knowing, and then you understand which labels you want to show, and which labels you want to hide.

The Awakened One you are, understands only that you are the child, as your human nature, until you become what you are as 'That One'. You can never have true Freedom until you allow the labels you are to fall from you as identity, and simply allow the treasure that each experience is to be the opportunity to embrace. All you are ever required to do is *embrace*.

That which you are, as a Christed One, is one who Embraces. That One does not say, "If I am this, think this, feel this, then I must be a ..." and then the label. For that One does not journey the thoughts and feelings, it simply experiences them in honesty, and in that, enjoys the Power that is the acknowledgement of Life. To speak in humility, "I am that which appears before me, that is the Within of me."

The Christ does not have an attitude that seeks to alter or change or deny. It has the understanding that that which It is as the existing one of Truth means that as journey and experience, there will be much that is come upon, much that is created, which does not have the approval of the conditioned world in which you live, as a human. But the Mind of the Christ does not breathe in the winds of any culture. It does not believe in the truth of any society. And it does not have to rationalize its existence in order to please Itself or anyone else. So, that one is free to roam upon a world that will feed it foods of thought and feeling. And the Christ walks amidst the destiny of man, the destiny of woman, and displays its Power, as the everlasting Life of Acceptance and Self-Acceptance.

The human journey, the human landscape, is to this one a vision of the soul, and so this one speaks, "Let me place in you an understanding that will register sense in the human mind and the human heart. You are, as human, your soul's expression. You are your Christ's dream." And so now, as this dialogue, you have come upon a path—your path—that speaks to you in terms of who you will become and who you are becoming, as the Christed One.

You live now in a world in which this Wisdom wants you to realize that there is more to your existence than your soul expression. You are the Dream of the Great One. And that means you are good and perfect in that Dream. You have always been the Allowance of the Christ you are. For *in* that and *as* that, you will now want to move more and more into greater and greater understandings. You will want to release yourself from the damnation of judgment that speaks,

"For what I am and who I am, I am lesser."

No, you are not. everything is in perfect order. You must simply ride the wave of every experience as if you were the simple taster of a beautiful wine. You are the connoisseur of your own existence. And you will

You are your Christ's Dream

understand everything about you, when you treat your life, like a wine connoisseur with a precious wine. Nothing is spoken in judgment, only in description, only in the feeling and the thought. You are here to acknowledge yourself as who you are in every circumstance.

You live beyond this Dream as that which is already the bearer of all great Truth. You are simply here to register Truth. That is the simple task of, "I am this. I am that." Not as a label, but as the sweet breath, that is blown in your face to smell and to taste. And you bow to your greatness that brought it to you and you to it, as experience. You bow to your own beauty. You respect that which is your life, for it is grand and magnificent. And now you will walk upon your life path with more knowing and more feeling.

There is only one champion of 'your cause' and it is you. You are the one who knows the path you are upon, and you can see it clearly. And in that you can be the one who approaches it all within the light of appreciation and embrace. So too, you will go forth upon your life path, moving into the Consciousness of that One, the Blessed Christ that you are.

I love you.

So be it.

The Center of the Crossroad

My Beloved One,

All thanks is given to those who, with great care and understanding, have come forth to be the Light in a world that seeks the Light in every way, on every day. There is so much to be thankful for, so much when observed, must be called brilliant, for it has allowed a great Shift to occur in the space of a small amount of time. A Shift so significant, that the future of humanity now holds a different hue, is focused upon a different identity, is embarking upon another destiny.

All that you have observed, and are observing, is a statement that is telling you to be single-minded in your own intent to contribute to, and be a part of, the evolving changes. You do not have to await any new or different instructions. The direction to go is inside you. It is a felt thing. And it is speaking to you clearly of your great desire to hold to what is most caring, and hold to what is most considerate. Hold to what is your own preferred way of being. This will affect others in their desire to live what they feel.

The surprising thing for so many is that the feelings you now have may not have been so obvious to yourself or your family, to your friends and neighbors *before* now and for some, *even* now. And you realize as we speak that somehow you have undergone an elemental shift in your focus of awareness. And it feels more like it happened to you than anything else.

How did it happen to you? This is the real question. It is the tantalizing puzzle. It is almost as if you went to sleep and awakened differently. All of those experiences are valid, in the sense of how you understand the experience. As night fell upon humanity, there was the slipping away, through dreams in the night, to a world you live within, and a 'you' that lives within that world. As the sun rose and a new day dawned you awakened to another world. And you that lives within this world is another 'you'. You and your world, in a dance of synchronicity, pirouetted, bowed, and turned the dance in another direction, into another expression and now for you all, another experience.

You—and your world—have been living upon a precipice for some time now. Holding onto your life in a precarious way, knowing inevitably that a time, a moment, would come when the balance would imperceptibly alter. But it was enough. Enough to set in motion the inevitable and unchangeable momentum, over the edge and into. That is what awaits you now. That is what has happened to you already. That is what is happening to you right now.

You did not dream a dream that you awakened from in fright, screaming. You did not have a nightmare,

The Center of the Crossroad

you simply passed yourself, as if in flight, upon a glorious Sky road: one of you leaving, one of you entering. Are you still you? Yes, you are. In fact, more you than you have been. Your world allowed you to undergo an immense and significant shift.

The calamitous events in your world distilled for you, in the eyes of your mind, in the eyes of your soul, in the emotions of your heart and the Spirit of your soul, as you watched through eyes of great perception the collapse and the falling downwards, inevitable, heavy, so heavy. And then, as if they were never held here at all, like a wind that blew, there were so many that traveled upwards to the Sky roads, into Heaven's Realms. Saints they were. Beings of Light they were. Gatekeepers for you, they were. For in their arising, they opened the Doorway through which poured forth a great Light of Awareness and Truth.

And the events of that day gave to you your world that fell over the precipice. And it gave to you the new dream that took flight as the old fell. You are joined for eternity now. You that remains upon your Earth, and those whose destiny it was to open the Doorway of Light. That too, was destined to open on that day. All true greatness, that is Change, holds within its very essence, two essential ingredients: death and birth. They are not separate but the same, even though to you it is as if one follows the other, one precipitates the other, one is the forerunner of the other. Even though your precious world of time allows you this perception of Truth, there is a far more explicit understanding you may draw on at this time.

Change of itself is another word for Life. In Truth, the two words are interchangeable. They are the within and the without of each other. They are part of the great Truth that speaks of momentum and movement. You understand those words in a human way, from the 'scientific', to one of simple observation. Movement and momentum are so essential to Life and Change that you mostly take your legs for granted. And the constant focus you have upon transportation and all its associated industries and necessities. The kaleidoscopic vistas available for you to appreciate and experience are all possible through movement and momentum.

You call these experiences, your world, your country as a nation, your neighborhood and your Mother Nature. Then there are the microbial worlds that are invisible to your human eye, but through eyes that science has created you can journey into those minute worlds of wonder. So, you already have a great appreciation of movement and the wonder that it produces and allows for.

There is a further understanding of movement and momentum that is more subtle, and it exists within what has just been described, and it exists beyond what has already been spoken of. The movement of consciousness called awareness, the movement within consciousness that propels awareness into arenas of

The Center of the Crossroad

feelings, thoughts, and visions not entertained before. Within consciousness lie all visions, all panoramas, all Life. Not just Life as we have entertained earlier, but Life that is beyond what your human mind will allow you to understand and describe. Beyond your ability to presently imagine.

If you were to simply exist as consciousness you would be faced with the ever-present feeling called *moment*. Momentum is movement, that is expansion, and you can expand into the infinitely small or the infinitely large. This expansion as momentum is the desire to know, to be, to exist as. It is, as desire, "I must be, I must do, and I must have."

So the process of experience, of education, of knowledge, of knowing, of seeing, of hearing, of tasting, of feeling are all a process of movement and momentum. You cannot begin to understand yourself in your world without knowing of movement and momentum. This allows you to understand coming and going, moving *to* somewhere, moving *from* somewhere, being in and getting out, up and down, yesterday and today, today and tomorrow. All of these concepts will have a physical worldly understanding as time and as the more subtle awareness — as understanding — of life and death, death and birth, beginnings and endings, endings and beginnings that are also governed by Time.

For all there is a climactic moment. It is never always known or appreciated unless it is of its very nature significant to you in your world. Significance may be self-granted or it may be thrust upon you, in your understanding. And even then there is not the separation of involvement that your world grants it. Instead, there is within Consciousness, as movement and momentum, forces, that you are a part of always, even though events may grant you distance from calamity and therefore safety to you as human body, human life. But beyond that, you are as much in the eye of the encounter as anyone who walked from this world into the next, as life encountering Life in an ongoing way.

You have, as consciousness, been through a death and a birth. And you have come to this moment as inevitably as you walk one foot in front of the other. The dilemma faced by many is that your daily life of movement has within it a level of habit. And in habit there is a sense of not having to be fully present, fully aware. Of being on automatic pilot, of doing it with your eyes closed, so to speak.

This is an intrinsic part of human life that sees routine as essential to self-management and self-regulation, and in that the sense of having an organized and controlled existence. Both of which are part of the process you call meeting goals. Meeting goals and human life are the advancement of you and your life upon a perceived pathway of greater and better. This can include health, wealth, and happiness to use one of your own catch cries. For those who seek to

The Center of the Crossroad

understand more of themselves and Life, there are many avenues, as spiritual, that you may take to grant yourself that same desire for *greater* and *better*.

What is the same, though, is the understanding that you must want within yourself as focused intent, as thought, as feeling, as the creation of a dream, and a vision of what you want to manifest. So upon your Earth there exists a Dream. And at this time, there are sufficient numbers of humanity, who as a collective consciousness, have called out from within themselves, from within their dream,

> *"Peace, peace, peace."*

And the movement is such that what is one person's dream, becomes another's. What is a husband's dream is now becoming his wife's dream. What is the mother's dream is becoming the son's dream. The daughter's dream is becoming her friend's dream. What is one family's dream is becoming the dream of another family. What is one community's dream is becoming the dream of many others. What is many nations' dream is becoming a dream for the whole world.

So this Dream now has momentum, has gathered power, and focus through the saturation of a 'dream' called war, called them and us, called better than, called competitiveness, called fear, called intolerance, called lack, lack of love and appreciation, lack of inclusion, and lack of sharing called greed. Greed that speaks,

THE WRITINGS

"I want what I want."

Blindly, ignorantly, selfishly and uncompromisingly, all of this is a description of the state of awareness, as consciousness, in which you as human speak and you spoke,

"This is who we are. This is who I am. This is life in our world. It will never change."

To understand the inevitability of Change is to contemplate the Light and the Dark of your world. One always follows the other. One anticipates the other. One bows to the other. The Circle of Life, as this movement, will continue to exist anywhere there is complacency, where there is compromise that is inherent in the sleep of habit and routine. Change will always be change. Movement will always be movement.

Humanity now exists at that Crossroad.

And at this moment, that is called the Center of the Crossroad, Change happens. It is the calling for peace. The calling for greater Life pulled you through the Crossroad. And at that pivotal moment, the past and the future were as one. At that moment, past and future existed as an equal power, each the epitome of Life calling to Life, from 'the within' of It and 'the without' of It.

And *to* your human eyes, *through* your human eyes, you spoke. "It is me. No, it is me."

The Center of the Crossroad

Which consciousness will you embrace, as Life, on the other side of the Crossroad? And it was already destined, from before that moment, that peace would emerge from the Crossroad, as that which is born, as that which is now the focus of the movement and momentum of Life.

And war, which has existed in the minds of humanity for so long now, as the consciousness of inevitability about human life, dreamed its final great dream as an expression of movement and momentum, of Change, of Life. For that is the consciousness of the inevitability of death, of pain and suffering, of victor and vanquished, of gain and loss, of fear and uncertainty. And so night fell upon an 'old' world and the sun rose upon a 'new' world.

Peace is the Life you live within, as consciousness, now. All uncertainty experienced by anyone at this time, is simply the smoke and dust at the Crossroad that has still not settled for many. And so their vision of the result is still not clear. Do not be afraid. Focus on, and celebrate, the birth of peace upon your world. Remain conscious and active in your embellishment of this consciousness. Speak words of peace to everyone. Think thoughts of peace to everyone.

"I want only the very best for you."

And let that thought entertain in you visions of how magnificent every precious life can be—how happy and fulfilled each life is—and how happy that makes you, in return.

THE WRITINGS

Continue to build the movement and momentum of peace within your families and all your churches, temples, and mosques, and upon all the lands, through all the rivers and upon all the oceans, amidst the forests of green and the plains of the wind walkers. And in the valleys below and upon mountains on high, speak of all Life as sacred and precious. Speak of the One Life that you are all sharing, that you are all a part of, as a human being, as a human expression, as your human experience.

But do not stop there, for those whose reach can go further, continue to dream dreams of lasting peace. Fill that peace with visions of what is greater for you and your world. Let Life inspire you with how much you can give to It, and how much Life can give to you. Sing songs of joy, dance the dance of rapture, and speak words of love.

You will be amazed at what was seemingly so lofty and ethereal, that was too much of Heaven's world and not human life. You will find that Heaven and Earth are reaching for each other and are entering a sweet and lasting embrace.

You, my beloved one, will bring the world of Heaven to this Earth. And you will bring this Earth to the world of Heaven.

I love you.

So be it.

"I Am the Center of Life"

My Beloved One,

Temptations come in many different forms. You are constantly being tempted, as an offering, to go in a certain direction, to take your life path, on any given day, in any given moment, in a particular direction, as experience.

Temptation comes as a desire, in which you are looking to experience particular feelings. Temptations are always about the Felt. Temptation is always indicating to you that the Felt is the foundation of all Life journeys. It does not matter what the mind creates as the play to journey within, it is always the Felt that propels it. The Felt is the engine that drives all experiences whether you have judged them to be desirable or undesirable.

Within the unawakened state and the awakening state, the Felt holds all of your human emotions. Your human emotions are not the State of the Felt, but they utilize its life force energy to express all of the differing human emotions. And in many cases to not express or even acknowledge feeling certain emotions, or for some, any emotion at all.

THE WRITINGS

Why is the Felt experienced in this way as your 'only human' self? The Felt is the Truth of you. It is the deepest State of your Being, whether it be human expression or Divine expression. The Felt is the Beginning State of Love. The Felt, as Love, never changes. It has never changed. It is an eternal State of Beginning, and as the Unchangeable it has birthed the Felt as the Changeable within all states of Time.

Within the realms of the Changeable there is, within time and space, Creation — all Creation — that is called form. Your world of matter is simply one expression and one experience of form. One experience and expression of the Changeable, within the realms of the Changeable. Your human emotions are an experience of this Creation as the time flow you call Earth. On this plane you have a variety of emotions that exist as this level of consciousness of the Felt. It is important that you hold fast to the awareness, that all of your human emotions, as changeable, are deriving the energy for their expression and experience from only one beginning Energy. An Energy that is called Love. So, you may understand that every single human emotion is held in Love, by Love, as Love, as the Felt, as the Beginning Creator Creation Life Force that has birthed all Existence.

The Felt is the primordial Energy, as Source Life Force, that has held, is holding, and will always hold all 'thought' creations. All thought requires the Felt in order to create any creation. In poetic terms of

"I am the Center of Life"

relationship endearment, The Felt is The Mother, the Womb, the sacred Yoni. The Thought, the pure Thought is The Father, the Protector Provider, the sacred Lignum. Together, as The One, there is Father as pure Thought and Mother as pure Desire, as the Felt. Together, merged, they are the Great Spirit of The One, as all Life, all Existence.

This Great Spirit is the pure state of Balance and Harmony. The Felt is harmonized as Love, pure Love. Pure Thought is harmonised Creator. Together, each is harmonised within the other as symbolised as the yin and yang, yin Mother, yang Father, yin the Felt, yang pure Thought, yin Surrender, yang Creator Power, yin Momentum, yang Movement, yin Desire, yang Action, and yin the sacred Yoni and yang the sacred Lignum.

Within the Felt, as the Felt, is the Erotic. The Erotic is the state of the Felt as Source. Erotic is the pure State of Surrender. It is the Pure State of Desire. The Great Spirit, as The One carries the Erotic, carries Surrender and carries pure Desire. This Great Spirit lives within all your creations of manifest life, whether you can, or will, acknowledge this within your conditioned state of judgement. Gratitude and appreciation are your happiness and joy, as Love coming forth as excitement and fulfilment with what the Great Spirit has brought forth as your co-creation.

Everything in your life is a co-creation of your thought emotions as conditioning and indoctrination, and as the pure Desire, pure Thought as the Great Spirit that is only Love. Your life is a manifestation of this Union Consciousness. It is seated within you and all around you unacknowledged consciously, except in those moments when true heartfelt gratitude and appreciation touches you, and then fills you, and overwhelms you, as your awareness. This is a level of purity you are experiencing as the Felt. It is Union Consciousness you are experiencing as the Felt in which you are Surrender. And it feels delicious, sweet and beautiful. This is who you are, in a pure State of Existence. This is you in Oneness Consciousness.

This is the Love Affair of The One, as The One, in The One. You are there, you are *in* that Love Affair, *as* the Love Affair. This is where you will find your desired states of ecstasy and bliss. This is where rapture, as a Divine state of Consciousness, is sourced. You cannot have rapture unless you are journeying the Felt as Surrender.

Surrender, to your human mind, creates fear, as the loss of identity, the loss of, "who I am" and the loss of all that you have constructed as personal self that you use to perform your life. Surrender suggests to this state of mind emotion self that there is a 'death' involved. There is a process of dying that has to be journeyed. And this is true, it is real, for the human ego consciousness must be let go of in order to incorporate the new consciousness, that is your True Nature ego Self. Ego, as 'I am', is always with you as

"I am the Center of Life"

you awaken, as your enlightenment and as your illumination. But it is not the human 'ego' that is a personal survival consciousness and, therefore, is focused on 'me' as its central focus. This consciousness sees itself as the sun in its own solar system, poetically speaking.

As you awaken, that focus changes, shifts, alters, to include other relationship connections as, "I am." The higher the state of awakened consciousness, the greater the relationship connection as, "I am."

Survival is so powerful, as a focus of consciousness, because in the deepest recesses of that consciousness is held helplessness, as not powerful or without power. So, the human ego consciousness is one that lacks power. It lacks the knowing of Power and the experience of Power, both of which are Divine in origin. To not know Power means 'power' must be created. Power, in order to be created, requires journey. Journeying life to become powerful does not always guarantee success. When success is not guaranteed it means that you must construct an 'edifice' of power around you and, from within that, perform actions that are perceptions of what the human mind declares to resemble power. To resemble power is to mimic Power. To mimic Power, it has to be constantly worked at. It has to be protected. To protect it, it must be projected.

You live in a world where every human, without exception, who is unawakened must play this game.

Because there is no individual autonomous Divine Knowing of "I am Powerful," alliances must be formed, and are formed, to create a collective of "I am powerful." This is all Survival Consciousness, whether you are within a collective that is an expression and experience of, "I am, we are, powerful," or a collective that wants the experience of powerful as, "I am, we are," but is not committed to creating the experience. So great is their mind and heart of conditioning, and indoctrination within the consciousness of lack, of not deserving and the inbuilt lethargy that will not allow the collective to truly create the experience of, "I am, we are powerful."

This is the 'play' that is now being visibly portrayed for all humanity to see, and witness, and experience personally. The understanding, as appreciation for truth, is that the collectives which are projecting, "I am, we are powerful," are as consciousness, no more powerful than you are. They have simply constructed and performed the collective edifice of, "I am, we are powerful." Your political, financial, social, cultural societies are their edifice of, "I am, we are powerful."

In order to sustain this, laws must be put in place, religion and education must be handed to you in a form that will keep you always conflicted about the morality of 'power'. Religion says do not aspire to be powerful. Education says that you can work to become a version of powerful that we will allow, and you will accept. In such cases you are being groomed from the

"I am the Center of Life"

moment the body is born, to accept this, as the way life is. In such a scenario there is hardly ever a questioning of this as, "Can life be expressed and experienced differently?"

This is always an 'awakening' thought; one that is outside of what is planted in your consciousness as part of your grooming from birth. Much of humanity is now experiencing 'awakening' thoughts. They are questioning their grooming, awakening to its purpose and intention. Awakening to the presence of the collective that has manifested an "I am, we are, powerful," version of Survival Consciousness. Awakening to a conscious consideration of the personal value to their experience of life, and the worth, as quality of life, that has been—and is—the grooming of you.

Awakening is not by accident. It is not because of what is happening as 'appearance' in your world. This is secondary. It is the result, the reaction, it is not the trigger, and it is not the provocation. Surrender is the trigger. Surrender is the provocation. Surrender as the Great Spirit in Consciousness. Surrender that is the Unchangeable Presence within all higher consciousness. Surrender that is now present on your world as Super Consciousness. Surrender that is Union Consciousness. Union Consciousness that is the pure essence of Oneness, which your human tongue would speak as "I am, we are, one."

Your quest, as your awakening, is to solve your

THE WRITINGS

personal riddle of Separation and Surrender. Your, "who am I?" held within your soul is rooted in this riddle. And the riddle cannot be solved without entering the Circle of Life. You are looking for this Self, as your True Nature, as essential to your spiritual awakening. This Self is the embodiment of the riddle, of Separation and Surrender.

Separation Consciousness as 'only human' is not the separation that is you as a Divine Sovereign Being. Sovereign and Union Consciousness are the Truth held within Oneness. Sovereign is held by Permission and Allowance within The Beginning as, 'I Am'. In order to be sovereign, the human self must release 'I am not sovereign'.

The dilemma for you as human is that you believe that your consciousness of, 'it's all about me', is you existing as a sovereign being. 'It's all about me', is survival, not sovereignty. Survival says surrender must be forced. So, 'it's all about me', is a battle, a fight, that is always being waged so that you do not have to surrender. Where surrender speaks of having to let go of something in yourself that you want to hold on to — whether it is a belief, an idea, a principle, an attitude, an action, a thought, or an emotion — all of this 'letting go' is your version of life as struggle. So, surrender means compromising something in you or about you that you are holding to as a perception of, "This is me, this is who I am."

You can begin your path of awakening with all of this

"I am the Center of Life"

in place as personal identity. This is a universal starting point for every human who begins a path of spiritual awakening. And Surrender partners you in your awakening from this very first moment. No matter how many lifetimes you have journeyed—"I want to awaken spiritually"—each one will begin anew with Surrender partnering your attachment to your state of ignorance, as personal consciousness.

Surrender sits as invitation, as the Felt, within you as another consciousness, another level, another layer, more refined, simpler and purer, waiting for you to pass through the Gateway. Surrender is The Mother Goddess Gateway in Consciousness. To approach this Gateway, a man must be the presence of personal transformation. He must undergo his own personal experience of inner great Change. He must reinvest his awareness with the desire, gifted to him from within the Felt, to merge, to become one with. To begin the remembering of the Love Affair, the lovemaking that is the Felt as Union Consciousness, surrender is the Gateway, the Entranceway.

In Eastern mysticism it is the sacred Yoni. Man must have already entered upon a personal pathway of rediscovering the meaning of the sacred Lignum. This is where change lies for each man as his journey into spiritual awakening. This is the sacred state that man must hold in order to approach the Mother Goddess Gateway and then become aware of being invited, drawn in, to the sacred Yoni. This will, in time, awaken

THE WRITINGS

the Path of the Erotic, as the Journey Home.

For Woman to approach and enter this Gateway of Remembering she must return to her True Nature as the Divine Feminine. She must remember the mystical nature of the sacred Yoni, must return to her true power as Surrender. You, as Woman, must come to terms with an already existing powerhouse of perceptions and beliefs around the word 'surrender'.

You must accept that you do not really know the Truth of the Divine Nature of Surrender, because it cannot be felt within Separation Consciousness. As 'only human' you are conditioned and indoctrinated to hold your consciousness within the 'them and us' battle for survival. The battle between the sexes, but equally important the battle within yourselves as womankind.

Separation Consciousness as 'only human' will never let you Be, which is your True Nature, within which exists the essence of your power as Mother Goddess. Life here, on your world, is a deliberately designed distraction, which is now being played out on a world stage. Chaos is the very root of the Distraction. Chaos that speaks, "There is no Divine plan. There is no Divine order. There is no Home you came from, as Divine origin." You are 'only human'. This, as a created way of life, a created meaning of life, destroys your desire to focus on your Centredness, which is different, as experience, as Consciousness, for man and woman, male aspect of the soul, female aspect the soul, Divine Masculine, Divine Feminine.

"I am the Center of Life"

Yes, as Woman, it is easier you say to go for the goal that your indoctrination and conditioning have steered your consciousness towards and into. Yes, it may appear easier, but you know that in truth it is a struggle. A struggle that overflows into all areas of your life. Why? Because in essence your nature is to flow and so there are no real boundaries for you as consciousness.

The essential nature of the Divine Feminine and, therefore, the female Essence of your soul is your 'juiciness'. This is not a sexual reference; it is a consciousness understanding. It is what is called your magnetism. And your magnetism insinuates the presence of something more, something deeper. It is the presence of Mystery. Mystery insinuates the presence of the Unfathomable, that is the Infinite, without beginning, without end.

A woman may look everywhere to find her centre and never find it, because her centre is the whole of her being. It is everywhere, *in* all things, *as* all things. This is The Mother you are. As human woman you have a version of self that is separated from your consciousness of, "I Am the Centre of Life." All ego human expressions and experiences of this Essence are aberrated and misdirected as performance and expectation. It is so easy for a woman to get completely lost in her human sensory mind emotion and spirit experience of The Mother, of the Goddess.

When looked at, as a comparison, the world of male

Essence looks far easier to go after and incorporate yourself in, as Essence. But it is not who you are. You can never win by taking on his Essence as a pathway for your fulfilment. What you believe you will gain is illusionary. There is nothing that you will take with you, as enlightened, to the 'other side'. And nothing that will be useful to your awakening in this or any lifetime. The prize of such a journey is the learning of what you are not. You are not male in essence; you are not the simplicity of that consciousness. And yes, you can judge it to not be fair. "How is it that man gets to have it so easy?"

As Goddess, Mother, you want him to be 'easier'. You are not looking to create a version of you as Mother, all Life, but a reflection of The Father, Pure Thought, as Lord, as man. Pure Thought that became Will, that became Purpose that became doing, that you speak of as journey. The Mother journeys through The Father. Goddess originally journeyed through Lord God. And in many cultures and civilisations woman has journeyed through the man. You perceive them as roles that have been played out, the role of man, the role of woman. But it flows much deeper than that trivialization of the Divine Essences of The One.

In times gone by, traditionally, the woman, the mother, was the centre of home life. She did not work as the man did. Her work was to Be. To be the epicentre of the home life. Even in indigenous cultures, the man was the primary hunter. He left the

"I am the Center of Life"

camp in search of game. The women in these cultures certainly were gatherers, but that positioned them around the village, the campsite, never far away from the children and the elderly. All of this is as expression, sourced within the Essences of The One, we refer to as The Mother The Father.

The 'play of life' in these times is about disrupting this harmony, this balance. And each of you, as man, as woman, can discern for yourself whether the created changes to the original Essences of The One, in your own lives, has given you a greater harmony and balance. Was the purpose to create harmony and balance and a greater level of fulfilment or not? In these times careers are seen as the path to fulfilment, even if it is inexorably bound to economic survival. So, you may ask yourself, is this true fulfilment or expedient fulfilment?

Anything, as lifestyle journey, that takes from you the Spirit essence of who you are is not serving your highest good or your highest purpose. Your societies and cultures, through forces of economic necessity, have dislodged you from your Spirit roots and foundations. In doing so, there can be no true inner peace or happiness. There cannot be true Fulfilment as is held within you as Mother Goddess creator creation.

Upholding the existing economic financial juggernaut is not the Beauty of your creator creation powers and will never be. For your Spirit powers are centred, as you, in the Preciousness of all Life. Your world economics are sourced in greed, in 'them and us', in a less-than and better-than 'reality'. None of this, as energy, as vibration, can sustain you in your pure Spirit Self, as Mother, as Goddess. It will destroy — and is presently destroying — you and your potential to awaken spiritually. For you to not have spiritual awakening, as an intention in this lifetime, will give the Dark Agenda exactly what they are aiming to achieve. No Golden Age, no Great Awakening, no Great Shift in Consciousness, and no Divine Mother Pre-eminence as Super Consciousness.

You are Her emissaries. You vowed to undertake this task, this journey, as part of your own greater spiritual awakening and the awakening of humanity. Your world is undergoing Transformation, and it is now important that each of you, as expressions of the Divine Feminine, undertake your individual transformations and return yourselves to the consciousness of Self Goddess as your own Beingness.

In this, the Preciousness of all Life has a greater possibility to be birthed as reality on this Earth plane.

I love you.

So be it.

The Instinctual You

My Beloved One,

It may be unusual for you to pay extraordinary attention to all that is occurring in your world right now. It is not unusual, however, to be of the understanding that what has come about is because you have found it necessary to either agree or disagree with current views and current attitudes that purport to herald in the new times, new views, new awareness and new understandings.

You cannot manipulate your own worldview beyond the combined understandings of what you already understand and what is offered to you for further consideration. You can compute an advancement of your own realizations in this way, but there will be limits to your awareness when using this approach.

"But what else is there?" you may ask. "How else is there to do it?"

As human, you must rely, it is said, upon these techniques because there are no other means through which you can arrive at expanded awareness. All other approaches are seen to be beyond the realms of what is normal. You cannot augment the challenge to anything presented to you, by your world, without the realization that you must accept the designated parameters of human mind, human intelligence. You will find yourself in the middle of an ocean of doubt, if what is portrayed as informational perspective comes from an unrecognized valid source, or an unacceptable method of gathering.

You live in a world where what is gathered, what is held and retained, and what is transmitted comes to you through the medium of the mind. The mind that is human. None of this is flawed. Indeed, it is by design. It can be said that this is what it is to be human. It is, however, unusual in another 'world' to function in such a way. You may argue about the relevancy of this given that you live in a world where to be human is the whole point of your existence. To experience your world using the human mind and human heart is the whole point. If it is not the point, then why do you have them?

Such logic, such understanding, is what allows this to continue as the norm. To be within this understanding creates its own reinforcement as normal, and its own quizzical-ness as a reaction that anyone would presume to bring something so basic, so normal, and seemingly natural into question. And that is the very point, for it is within this presumption that the great 'sleep of ignorance' is allowed its existence. Ignorance—as being basic, normal, and natural—is what is being upheld. Such upholding allows the process of information gathering to be seen as the way out of ignorance. Where ignorance, as what is *not* known, is measured in terms of what is *possible* to be known, what *must* be known, and equally what is *yet* to be known.

However, knowledge that is informational, suffers from attention to detail because it cannot be held onto as a forever known unless attention to its detail is constantly adhered to. If you lessen or let go of anything in the mind of 'attention to detail' it will, in time, become forgotten or lost. The details will become hazy and not easily recalled. You will become frustrated with yourself for not remembering, and with your inability to fully recall it. Such experiences are life for you as human. And, although accepted, it is not without annoyance that it has to be this way. So once again the question can be asked,

"Does it have to be this way?"

Yes it does if you are to involve yourself in knowing that lives through the human mind and the preferences of the human heart, the human soul. Is there a point in bringing to your attention any alternate possibility? Is this possibility feasible and open to the human people at large? It is good to have such questions?

Let me ask you a question. "Does humanity want this to be the way, or does it want something different?"

If humanity is happy to accept this process as 'the

way', then it will remain the way. And so all that is associated with this process will also remain, as aspects of the way life is. Institutionalized learning, newspapers, magazines, libraries and the media, all of them are tools of this way. The acceptability of this way is held as reasonable, as possible, as an 'only', because from within these experiential parameters there are no other possibilities. However, if you were to consider a world that looks like your world: a world of land and oceans, valleys and mountains, beaches and reefs, trees and rocks, rivers and streams filled with life, life upon the earth and within the earth, life in the skies and the waters — this is already familiar to you. It is already an accepted part of the tapestry of life, the way of the human.

What if all of that remained as it is visually to you, so that you, to all appearances, seemed to be in familiar surroundings? But what if you looked more closely? What if you stopped for a moment and you actually began to breathe to, and become connected to, all that you took for granted? And what if, in that, you became aware of different feelings inside you? You became aware of being not so brain-orientated, but rather awareness-orientated. And what if, in your state of natural intelligence, you were able to clearly distinguish between the two different focuses?

The mind, the brain, that you call human has given you a great and brilliant opportunity to arrange your world into a meaningful experience, an experience

The Instinctual You

that places you at the center of your world, the center of your life. Everything is viewed outwards through your eyes, your ears, your nose, your perceptions, your feelings. The centrist view of life, whilst great in its ability to grant you endless opportunities to understand life, also gives you endless opportunities to understand yourself.

The inter-relationship between you and your world is what has caused you to evaluate your significance and importance, your worth and value, your ability and desire to love and be loved. All of these have, in your understanding, made you and your life, outwardly and inwardly exactly the way it is. Because you hold this understanding there are overwhelming considerations that are now the bubble, the environment, you live within.

Inside every human there is a micro-environment, and that environment is for so many seen as being as uncontrollable as the weather is in your macro-environment. All attempts to manage and control the micro-environment bring forth your own sense of inadequacy. Just as you may attempt to control anything in life, you will not always know the outcome of your interference. You may project an outcome as part of your strategy to control, however, there are so many considerations that are at the effect of any single issue of control that as soon as you shift one of them it immediately alters an indefinable series of consequences. Which may not come into effect straightaway, but at some point down the road of your life, it will be played out as drama, as consequence, on the center stage of your life. Unless there are changes made as a result of considerations that lie outside the role of the human mind, but which must enter the human mind initially for consideration.

If you were to live your life more instinctively you would begin to appreciate that everything, absolutely everything, would move you in some way. Everything would affect you in some way. There would never be anything in life that you could shut down to. The Instinctual You is not a mind-centered you, it is a Life-centered you; and as such you are a constant play, direct, forthright, beautiful, brilliant, powerful, vulnerable and fragile; living on the edge of life in each moment, aware that life is the sweet breath you are, in that moment. It is the wind in your nostrils, it is life as aliveness, that is seen through your eyes in that moment. It is the sun, the rain, or the snow upon your body in that moment.

The Instinctual You is wild. Wild because it considers nothing, there is nothing to consider. There is only the moment, the point in which the whole of life is focused and you are — in the experience of that — aware, awake, alive, open, accepting and fluid. Nothing felt is questioned, subverted or suppressed, and none of it is exaggerated, dramatized or exploited in any way. It is a refinement, it is a naturalness, it is a preciseness, it is a perfect movement, a perfect response: never thought

The Instinctual You

about the moment before or the moment after, never felt the moment before, and only felt until it is done. It is never held on to, never toyed with or played with in order to evaluate yourself, anyone, or any other living thing, not Life, not God, none of it.

The human mind's contrived version of life evaluates everything, and in that everything is drawn into question. Everything, therefore, can be doubted for its intentions and its questionable involvement or lack of involvement. Hence, human life is extremely complex and immensely distorted. It is a fragmented view in which 'truth' is sought, and understandings where 'truth' is desired. As a maze it pretends to offer you its own way out. And it wants to keep you focused on the maze. It cannot offer you anything outside of the maze as a solution. So, life called 'human' is really a caricature of life. It is life in a bubble, separated from the opportunity to live life instinctually. Is it really possible to do that? To even ask this question, to pose it, to consider it, means you are clearly open to an alternative to your present worldview.

Such openness will also allow you to feel the freedom and power associated with the Instinctual You. You will also recognize, at least in some way, the barriers to moving from one experience of life to the other. You may already feel the powerful binding force called 'managing your life', where everything is closeted in some way, shape, or form. You may now be aware that this actually delays life, as aliveness, from arriving as an experience, as a moment, as a movement, as a truth with no past or no future.

What you realize is all of what must be dealt with, as your life, are the obstacles to becoming the Instinctual You, the Momentary You. And in that realization there is held the fear that you are without substance. To be unsubstantial is to fear not being known as self, and not being known by, or knowing of, your world. You are so free and so liberated as the Instinctual You that the whole meaning of life in your mind would feel disintegrative.

To prevent this madness from overtaking you and overwhelming you there is always a safety net called Will. It requires willpower, Divinely sourced and gifted to you, as the truly great key to any shift in consciousness, any shift in awareness. You cannot truly change anything without bringing Will to bear. So, any lack of Will, brought on by fear and uncertainty, prevents you from Becoming. So, you may feel safe and assured that all the time you want to take—in order to create opportunities for consideration and to take the baby steps that build confidence—is available to you. The confidence that is so essential to Will and the building of it as the Power of Change.

You may allow yourself as much time as you need to pay attention to the ever-present existence of a 'you' that is a contrivance of the mind and the time to play with, as awareness, even initially using your mind to

The Instinctual You

do it, the sense of who you would be as the Instinctual You. Never mind that you cannot be that one immediately. Instead, build a vision as thought and feeling, as awareness of that you. Call it forth, and allow the beliefs to diminish without question that you are what your mind says you are, or what your mind's feelings say about you, or what your feeling mind takes you through. All of it as an environment, the best and the worst, the great and the despised, and all that is mediocre, that is between these extremes, is a fabrication. All of it is a story.

Right now, the Instinctual Mind awaits you. And this Mind is not the mind of control. It is the Mind of Life. It is not the mind of judgment, but the Mind of Life. It does not rebuke you or your life. It does not view life as anything other than what it is as experience. The Instinctual Mind is the mind that does not question anything. It is the Mind that embraces all. It speaks about all. It announces all. It sees all as an experience of life. In these instances, it becomes a powerful exponent of you as soul. For it now aligns you to what comes from your soul to you. It aligns you, as soul to human-life you, without interference. Such greatness as this—for surely it requires greatness and brilliance to commence upon such a Path—will be recognized and understood by you, because you are no longer living like other humans.

You have become, and continue to become, a Wild One. And in that, not dangerous to yourself or others, although others may in your presence feel that wildness, and be inwardly disturbed by it. But that is good because disturbance is the possible onset of inspiration, and inspiration introduces the possibility of the new, and the new heralds the passing of the old. And in that there is movement, and in that there is change. Consciousness is served, Life is served, and you are both served and are serving. That is your greatness, that is your brilliance, and that is your life. You may pass from this world never realizing your dream to be the Instinctual You, but that does not matter. You will achieve it, for it is indeed your destiny within your Awakening to move back into your Instinctual body from which you departed as your mind became filled, and your karmas became you and your life.

To be the Instinctual One is to be the Innocent One. To be the Innocent One is to be, in your understanding, the child again. To be the child is to bow to the supremacy of the state of No Mind. That is not to say you will give away your intelligence, but that you will give back to intelligence its original environment of Peace and Love, of tolerance, forgiveness, and compassion. You will give it back to the State of Compassion. For it is in such an environment that the genius of the mind is birthed and will take flight. For now, it is as it has always been, it is connected to Life, as Life. It is no longer an instrument of separation as is the human mind, as is human intelligence; it is the Mind and Intelligence of the One. The One that is all

The Instinctual You

things from the Beginning, from which nothing can be added, and nothing can be taken away. It is the completeness. It is the whole.

You, my beloved, are already this and in your awakening you will remember what you have forgotten. You will know what is impossible to believe. You will create, even when you believe creation is not of your power in any way that you would define as substantial. Where, in this instance, substantial refers to your ability to create, that is outside of and beyond the understandings and limits of the human mind. But the human mind will always be your ally, in conjunction with the power of Will, to begin to open and experience yourself as Life without judgment or filters.

The Instinctual You is the crucial and important initiation and journey that your path will take on its way to full awakening. It is how you will know — and who you will become — as the mind and the heart of judgment falls away, and the Mind and the Heart of Life becomes you more and more. You are a brilliant journey, you are magnificent and great beyond your present ability to know, accept, and be. But it matters not, for you are on your way and you are upon your path. You will journey the highs and the lows of your path as you move from the depths of 'despair' and 'despise' within your human mind and heart to the heights of your experiences of Life as the Instinctual One, the Momentary One, the One that is both

THE WRITINGS

liberating and liberated. You are Life's treasure, and you treasure Life. There is nothing so important that it needs to be held onto or filed away for any future. Everything you experience is of equal value and, as such, is given to fully and totally, no matter what it looks like or what it feels like.

The Instinctual You does not have a repository of experiences, so what it looks like has no history, has no category or box in which it can be put in order to be recognized. You are as the moment, and in that you are a Living Truth, you are an expression of Life. *As* that, you are truly living, and *in* that, your life flows for there is nothing that creates a stuck-ness. And in that a solidness, which then becomes the personality identity, that in turn becomes your lifeline of hope. Hope that wants that identity to work for you in the world called your life, in which you are hoping to avoid life bringing to you that constant cycle of, 'maybe it will, and maybe it won't'.

The Instinctual Mind is not looking for anything other than more Life.

The beauteousness of any baby, any infant child, is the Lightness of Being they are as the Instinctual Self. When you next experience this in their presence, know that you have already been the Instinctual One in this lifetime. As you grew your stuck-ness, called personal identity, it became a solid definable you. As the Instinctual One you are not definable other than to speak about what is observed and experienced in any

The Instinctual You

moment. The lack of a rigid personality creates a beauty and an other-worldliness around you, and it is real because you do not live in the inner environment of the human mind heart. You live in the environment of Life, undisturbed, and you are pure, Pure Life.

Such is the path of awakening and, as such, it is a brilliance you are to return to. I bless your life and your path and the brilliant awakening you are becoming, and are to become.

I love you.

So be it.

The Power that is Love

My Beloved One,

The winds of change upon this world are having an enormous consequence in the lives of each human. And this is affecting, as influence, change upon all other life forms and life expression. You must be clear, definite, and as present as possible, in your determination of which movements are most important *in* your life, and *as* your life at this time.

Rebelliousness as a behavior, tantrums as emotional outbursts, and fear as rage and disorder within your own state of being become prevalent in your daily life if you attempt to distort the flow of input that is coming towards you. You may want to distract yourself in this way, but if you do then you and your life experiences will become more and more agitated. More and more compressed into the confines of your 'control' consciousness.

The sweet whispering winds of Love and Peace are a subtle presence now upon your world, emanating through the Australia Gateway, charging the lives of spiritualists everywhere on your Earth plane to meditate, pray, and chant within this sweet Wind. To imbibe it as the Breath of Peace, the Breath of Love

THE WRITINGS

within all your true sacred practices.

The mystical nature of this Australia Gateway is so profound, it must be experienced as personal awakening to truly understand and appreciate the enormity of the Consciousness that is flowing through it. And flowing into this world, this Earth, and all consciousness upon, within, above and below, and all consciousness to the north, the south, the east and the west. If you want this Love, if you want this Peace you must go for it. You must accept the challenge it represents to your current lifestyle and your current purpose in living.

The media of your world is now so intricately controlled that it is easy to believe that the divide called 'left and right' actually is your own truth, as reality. Everywhere the creation of the news as real, as true, as factual, is only truly food to feed the 'unawakened consciousness'. This is in the desperate hope that in doing so it will remain strong and needed by the mind emotions, and its physical body component to remain as the food that you are 'asleep' within, unconscious within. And your 'reality TV' now draws you emotionally, energetically to those 'realities', that continue to feed all of your inner beliefs about yourself and life.

No matter how you justify it all as entertainment, your comfort level within the drama is only a reflection of your own comfort levels within any of your personal beliefs about yourself and life. All of this, as 'old'

The Power that is Love

consciousness, is still today your present consciousness. And the powers that be, on every level and within every avenue of life, are strongly motivated to maintain you in this present consciousness in order for them to remain present as control, as power.

So much can be spoken of as the level of intimacy this power now has *in* your life, *over* your life. But this, as your desire to awaken, must motivate you to move beyond knowledge of any and all 'conspiracy theories'. As information they only feed in you your present nature as the 'old' consciousness, unless you are actively involving yourself in time-honored practices that center you as consciousness, as life. More in the 'new' consciousness, more in Love, more in peace and compassion, more in trust, more in happiness and joy, and more in gratitude and appreciation.

The consumer consciousness in your world was created for you out of greed, to involve you in greed as a consciousness of wanting. Endless wanting. Wanting that is to never be satisfied. So, it maintains you in the 'what about me' unfulfilled nature you derived, as your nature, as you awoke to the realization that Love as pure consciousness, Peace as pure consciousness, was not truly present as life, as experience, as expression upon this Earth.

So, the 'what about me' that began its life within you, through unfulfilled love, turned to consumerism as the great personal striving to feel fulfilled, to feel happy, to feel in that, lovable and even loving. But it is the great Distortion, and in that the great Distraction, that fills your life with mediocrity as an unwillingness, or even a perceived inability to go beyond the borders and boundaries of this level of living your life. Material comfort and ease is not being questioned here. For there is a remarkable and true difference between economic equality — as comfort and ease for everyone everywhere — and the controlling agenda of consumerism as consciousness.

To break free of this mold, as a lifestyle you are subjected to, is part of your awakening. It is part of your realization that such a pressure as mind emotion, and such a pressure as 'hunger consciousness', can never be saturated, it can never be satisfied. You can tell yourself you need this, and you need that. That you must have this, and you must have that, but the truth is you are being locked into the unconscious pattern of 'me and my life' which is only a sophisticated, complicated, and intricate version of survival consciousness.

It may not look like survival consciousness because, economically, your nation may be 'wealthy' and not of the third-world category. But that is the smoke-and-mirror trickery of consumer consciousness. It creates the appearance of being different to those less well-off economically, but the consciousness of survival is the same. You simply have more to choose from and acquire in order to feel you are adequately surviving. The fearful nature of such a consciousness is present everywhere within your culture.

Consumerism, as a system, is to give you a lifestyle and a purpose based within a controlled financial structure that oversees the consciousness of the 'marketplace'. So, those who control the financial system also control the consciousness of the marketplace, and ultimately and profoundly, control the individual human consciousness as your constant need to be involved in the marketplace for all of your needs and requirements. This is the present 'circle of life' consciousness that pulls you constantly away from your center as True Nature, as a spiritual being, who in essence is self-contained. The magnificence of your true being can only be experienced by returning to your center as pure, as Peace, and as Love.

There is the belief, as the 'old' consciousness, that everything must be 'fixed' for your benefit, everything must be 'prepared' for your benefit. In your unawakened state you believe and expect that you must be given to, that you must be 'fed'. You must be provided for, and so there must be a system of providing. This is the life system you exist within here on Earth. Everything is provided for you. This, you speak, is a good thing, a necessary thing and within your unawakened state this is understandable

But those whom you allow to provide for you, within such a state of consciousness, can then decide for you *what* to provide, *how* to provide, *when* to provide, *why* to provide, and *if* to provide. So, you are simply being led to consume their 'decisions' on what 'providing' will look like as your life and lifestyle.

In the unawakened state, this consciousness—as your beliefs—allows you to 'consume' understandings of self and life that you may choose to adopt as 'factual', as 'truth'. When, indeed, the 'provider' within the unawakened consciousness gives you what serves *their* interest in maintaining *their* power of influence as the 'provider'.

You cannot walk away from this as a real-life changing answer that will serve your consciousness of awakening. You must instead awaken whilst within it as knowing and as awareness. This is the true power of influence within higher and refined consciousness. You will not simply awaken yourself; you will—as a wave motion—ripple out as higher consciousness to the world around you, and that will build a bigger and bigger wave that will eventually move out across the whole of your world.

This is how the Great Shift will gain its power, momentum, and influence as humanity's awakening. Yes, it is a spiritual awakening, and you are a spiritual being having a human experience. And so, the more you awaken back into the spiritual being you are then the human experiences you desire as life and lifestyle will naturally change and elevate. So, the culture will change, the society will change, and in that each nation

The Power that is Love

will change. As personal 'identity' changes the national Identity must change, as a pure reflection.

This is why you must remember to stay focused on personal change. You will not change the national or international agenda, either as the 'up front' or the 'hidden', by ignoring your own agendas either as upfront or hidden. Only an unawaken consciousness can, as deflection, support the idea of a national or international change in consciousness without a personal change that would nurture it into existence.

So, this is not simply about new ideas to adopt as change. Ideas of themselves, although able to strike the chord of change cannot, on their own, orchestrate change as the power of change. This power is Love, only Love. All higher ideals and ideas for a better way of life, can only be birthed from the Womb of Consciousness as Love, within Love.

Only Love can presence itself in all Life, as Life. Only Love carries the Truth of all Life. Only Love, as essence, has the momentum required to penetrate the Divine Soul and trigger it as a homing beacon for your consciousness, calling you to move back into the magnificence you truly are as pure Love. So, your life must become more than ideals and ideas for a greater world. They must be given wings to fly and only Love can be those wings. Only Love wants to find a way, a path, that will be the vehicle you will utilize to implement personal change.

And as Love moves towards you, within you, to

become you, you must voluntarily decide to move towards Love. This begins the merging. And for a time, in the journey, there is the feeling of parallel lives, and both have a place within you, as you. This can be a topsy-turvy time in your life because you are still aligned, as self-recognition, as self-awareness, to the old consciousness as your unawaken human ego. But you are also awakening into your higher states as conscious Self. This is the Divinity you always are, in which you feel the Divine presence of forgiveness and compassion, of allowance and letting go, of permission and self-responsibility. Of wanting to know who you are as soul and the choices — as 'work to be done' — that you, as soul, have selected and elected to participate in as your present lifetime.

You must embrace the acceptance of being at a point in your life in which you want to taste all of the different flavors of consciousness within you, without judgement, with acceptance, as Love; that are the details of what to let go of, what to be released from, what to embrace as you, and what to look at again and see through new eyes: the eyes of gratitude and appreciation.

In sacred schools of learning, these practices — as your approach — have been called the Laws of the Universe. Not just this universe, but all universes. These principles, as grace and blessings, manifesting into thought form are expressions of Love. Held in the Light, as Light. And within the Light they are filled

The Power that is Love

with Love, as Love.

Thus, they are the Laws that govern all true Change. As the Laws they are Wisdom's Gateway and the Heart's Gateway into eternal Love, eternal Life. You must connect yourself to these Laws in order to awaken spiritually into your Truth as Divine Nature. These Laws represent life and death, to you as consciousness, for they carry the power that will require humility of you. Humility to bow to the realization of who you have become and who you truly are, in spite of what you have become.

Too little effort is the danger all awakening ones can be subjected to. And if you are an unawaken one looking at the possibilities for you, and your life, to include the Laws of the Universe as a consideration of how to, and why to awaken — then this is for you to contemplate as well. Love must, at some point, override all other reasons to awaken. For without Love you cannot truly awaken, and you can never fully Self Realize.

In the meantime, there are so many other concerns you can concentrate on without dealing with the central core of all Life, as Self Love. And that is quite normal and natural within the state of 'parallel lives', in which the human ego orientation, still tips the balance as life experience and life expression for you. Once again, the importance and significance of meditation — and within meditation, the Breath — must be handed to you for further consideration, further encouragement, to become your definitive statement of how to prioritize the time and effort you put into your awakening.

The Great Shift in your own personal life is your first priority. No matter what your dharma looks like as your 'highest' work in the world, it must always be fanned by the wings of Love, that wants the very best for everyone everywhere. And so, it is with the birthing of the Universal Consciousness, as humanity's consciousness, and the letting go of the 'what about me' and the 'all about me' consciousness of the human ego.

You are awakening the Universal Self, the Christ-Buddha Self, that is your true 'I am' as Love, only Love. To awaken fully, as the Christ-Buddha Consciousness, you must constantly be aware of the presence of your other life, your parallel life as human ego self. The depth and subtlety of the journey of unawaken ego, held as human soul, cannot be truly known. It cannot be given to you by anyone else, not even an Enlightened master or an Illumed Lord or Goddess. Only your personal journey of experience can place you inside the knowing of what it is you are still battling with. What you must once again bring the Laws of the Universe to, in order to dissolve the Ignorance into the Light of Love you are.

How you participate in this relationship with Self, as parallel, as dual, is a 'walk' you must constantly exercise along your path of refinement. You can be told of your current, 'sticking points' and that can help

The Power that is Love

you recognize what you are dealing with. But the energetic experience is yours alone to have, yours alone to master. Yours alone to become the Christ-Buddha Consciousness within, and then go beyond.

Always shifting, always moving, seeking out the awakening Gateways that will lead you to your next level of duality as the One Self. The dance of the Light and the Dark, of Realization and Ignorance, as your parallel lives, joined, yet separated by what you cannot yet understand as experience, as "who am I?" This 'wanting to know' is the Divine driving force that is constantly using the soul you are to presence the power of God in you, and to know all things as the Self you are.

Once this is awakened as the power that is Love within your soul, you must live your life accordingly. Even if you attempt to sabotage this soul resonation of awakening, you can never truly succeed. Even if in this lifetime, you may darken the corridors of Light that you have already walked within as consciousness, there will be renewed opportunities, as lifetimes to come, in which you can absorb yourself once again, as your duality, in your parallel lives.

And once again you will face choice. You will experience all of the hardness and softness within the conscious self, and you will stumble upon, you will open into, you will be gifted as karmic graces and blessings, the Laws of the Universe. And once again you must 'walk your walk of awakening and ignorance', and within it, uncover the state of Self Realization that is always with you, is always within you, as you.

I love you.

So be it.

Concerning the Author

The Authorship is unknown, but is held within the mystic symbolism of the Golden Bee.

The Golden Bee Enterprise has been created as the home of The Writings. A sacred sanctuary, and a tabernacle for the Divine who are the authors of this work.

The Golden Bee — as a symbol for the mystical significance of this Wisdom — holds the Divine Power of Mother Goddess. Calling to the Divine Feminine in the souls of all humanity, calling to the souls of man and woman alike, calling to the individual, and calling to the one family of humanity.

Within the mysticism of the Golden Bee is held Divine purpose, is held the instincts of the messenger, the servant *to* the Divine bringing to humanity Wisdom *from* the Divine.

Symbolically, mystically, The Golden Bee is The Mother, is Matriarchal, is Goddess, is Divine Feminine. As the Divine Mother it symbolizes family, unity, and working as one to bring forth fruitful prosperity and abundance equally for all. It is union consciousness that expresses teamwork and communication, industry, and self-responsibility.

Union consciousness is eternal and indestructible, opening you to every kind of miracle. Within Her golden glow you are offered the opportunity to find your own path, as unique contribution to a larger vision and purpose within a collective momentum in consciousness and purpose for a whole humanity.

The Golden Bee is a mystical symbol for the incoming Divine Mother flow as Super consciousness bringing to each soul the opportunity to embrace Great Change as it settles within the hearts and minds of an expectant humanity.

Acknowledgements

The Source of Consciousness that is expressed as the Wisdom that is The Writings is filled with gratitude and appreciation, as great Love, for all who have answered the call of their soul's destiny to be a part of bringing this Wisdom to humanity.

There are those Great Ones who as bodhisattva have quietly and anonymously, been instrumental in bringing forth the opportunity and the pathway for this Wisdom to emanate in this world in a form and expression that is palatable to humanity at this time.

There are those midwives, who, within the Womb of Mother Australia, have assisted in birthing The Writings for an expectant humanity of souls. To these ones a special thanks as heartfelt gratitude and appreciation goes to Deborah Fay, CEO of Disruptive Publishing. To her editor, Joanne Scott; and to Alicia Grady at www.struckbyviolet.com for the cover design. Also, for the audiobook a special thanks to Simone Feiler, owner and founder of Brisbane Audiobook Production.

Finally, a bowed and humble thank you to all who will discover this Wisdom and make it their own. It is your passionate insistence that this would be your time to

THE WRITINGS

catapult your consciousness into greater and higher states of soul evolution as your own spiritual awakening. Thank you. It is you who has called it forth as intention, and it is you who has manifested this as your personal outcome.

This is the power of Love in action.

Enjoy the fruits of your continuous spiritual awakening within the Wisdom that we have simply called The Writings.

On behalf of an awakening humanity, we thank each and every one of you.

What's next from the same Source?

There are more books to follow this one.

The Wisdom contained within this book is part of a collection that has been forthcoming since 1995 and continues to this day.

Why now?

Timing is everything. The gathering of this Wisdom was always to be the first step. Within the journey of the gathering, the destiny of this Wisdom was not always clear. So too, the timing in which it would be gifted to humanity.

With the birthing of the new yuga — the Sattva Yuga in 2024 — as the Yuga of New Beginnings, it has become obvious that the building of this body of Wisdom has always been for the purpose of assisting humanity in its Great Awakening into the Higher Consciousness as the Sattva Yuga, and to assist in the birthing of each soul's new beginning as personal spiritual awakening.

Contact Golden Bee

thewritings.au@gmail.com

thewritings.au

www.ingramcontent.com/pod-product-compliance
Lightning Source LLC
Chambersburg PA
CBHW060453090426
42735CB00011B/1972